THEY REMEMBER AMERICA

They Remember America: The Story of the Repatriated Greek-Americans

BY THEODORE SALOUTOS

UNIVERSITY OF CALIFORNIA PRESS
BERKELEY AND LOS ANGELES 1956

UNIVERSITY OF CALIFORNIA PRESS
BERKELEY AND LOS ANGELES, CALIFORNIA

CAMBRIDGE UNIVERSITY PRESS
LONDON, ENGLAND

COPYRIGHT, 1956
BY THE REGENTS OF THE UNIVERSITY OF CALIFORNIA
LIBRARY OF CONGRESS CATALOG CARD NUMBER 56-9300

DESIGNED BY WARD RITCHIE

TO THE MEMORY
OF MY FATHER AND MOTHER

PREFACE

The immigrant has played a conspicuous role in the social and economic history of the United States, and historians have given him much of the recognition he deserves. Unfortunately, very little has been written about the immigrant who has returned to his native land. This neglect of the repatriate is surprising, since the eastward movement to the European homeland has been going on for a long time and has involved large numbers of immigrants. Figures released by the United States Bureau of Immigration show that, over a twenty-four-year period, more than four million Italians, Englishmen, Poles, Greeks, Germans, and representatives of other nationality groups declared their intention of returning to their homelands. Hence an inquiry into the experiences and status of the repatriated seems appropriate, particularly at a time when both scholars and national policy-makers have been searching for evidences of American influences abroad.

The present inquiry has been limited in two ways. Its scope has deliberately been confined to one nationality group—the Greek-American. This limitation is intended to emphasize rather than to minimize the need for similar studies about other national groups, and to encourage other scholars to enter the field. What has been attempted with the Greeks can certainly be accomplished, perhaps more effectively, with the more numerous and hence more significant Italians, English, and Poles. The library and statistical resources of Italy and England, at least, should prove more rewarding than those of poverty-stricken Greece. The second limitation, that of the period of time covered, was largely determined by the numbers of Greek-Americans returning to their homeland in various years. Although the present study covers primarily the period from 1908 to 1924, it stresses the years immediately before and after World War I (1911–1914 and 1919–1921), when Greek repatriation was heaviest.

PREFACE

The absence of published historical studies dealing with the voluntary repatriation of the Greeks, or indeed of any immigrant group, has proved both an advantage and a disadvantage. It was advantageous in that I did not have to imitate the methods and procedures of earlier scholars, and disadvantageous in that I lacked the benefit of someone else's personal experience in the field. I was compelled to rely exclusively on my own resources. But the novelty of the subject fortunately presented fewer obstacles than I had originally anticipated. After some preliminary reading and probing, I drafted a tentative outline of my proposed project and submitted it to several historians for comment and criticism. All of them responded generously with useful suggestions and unstinted encouragement.

My research efforts were aided in another major respect. As a member of the Social Science Research Council Seminar on Cultural Exchange, whose chairman was Professor Franklin D. Scott of Northwestern University, I benefited from the interchange of facts and ideas contributed by the participants, all of whom were working in closely related areas. From these sessions came a broadened vision and a deeper insight, as well as practical suggestions for new techniques to be applied in the field.

I started my field work before I left the United States for Greece by availing myself of every opportunity to question and interview earlier Greek immigrants in the Chicago, Detroit, and New York areas. I wanted to get as many firsthand accounts of immigrant experiences as possible, even at this late date, and to absorb as much of modern Greek culture in the United States as I could before embarking for Greece. This early field work brought me into contact with persons representing many different ways of life: businessmen, both small and large, clergymen, journalists, consular and diplomatic officials, factory workers, shopkeepers, pensioners, widows, children of repatriated immigrants, and others directly or indirectly associated with my subject.

But my first real insight into the repatriated immigrant, as

PREFACE

distinct from the immigrant remaining in the United States, came with my voyage aboard a Greek ship, the *Nea Hellas*. Here indeed was a floating treasure of information. Most of the passengers were either Greeks returning home after a brief visit to the United States, or Greek-Americans traveling to Greece for short or indefinite stays. Interspersed among them were immigrants journeying to their native land for the sole purpose of repatriating themselves, and others making an exploratory voyage with the same thought in mind. Most of the passengers spoke Greek of varying quality, or dialects. Of the ship's company, almost everyone from the ranking officers to the deck hands was Greek. The cuisine was Greek, the temper of the officers was Greek. This setting gave me the opportunity to speak as much Greek as I cared to, and also to gain insight into the psychology of the returning Greek-American.

Like others aboard the ship, I wondered why people would leave the United States to live in Greece. After 1940 Greece experienced nine successive years of war, occupation, resistance, and civil strife. Although the guerrilla fighting had ended in 1949, less than three years before my voyage, reports currently circulating indicated that the physical and psychological impacts of the war were still widely felt in Greece. I lost little time in trying to discover the attractions this ravaged country held for its returning sons and daughters. On board ship I talked to persons going back to Greece for repatriation, hoping to learn their reasons for so doing. Although the back-to-Greece movement of the 1950's lay beyond the scope of my study, I was anxious to check a long-standing belief that modern repatriates felt the same motivations as the immigrants who returned just before and after the First World War. Subsequent research confirmed my hypothesis, and thus my own voyage to Greece served as a testing ground not only for my interviewing techniques, but for my theories as well.

I held my first conversation with a native of Thessaly who had recently been a grocer in western New York. After spending the war years in Greece, he had come to the United States in 1946, and now six years later was retracing his steps to his birthplace. He was returning at the insistence of his wife who, besides preferring the life and climate of Greece, wanted to be near her mother. Another Greek-American, after an absence of some thirty-five years, was going back to see children who were infants when he had left them, but who now had families of their own. An elderly gentleman, apparently in his late seventies, said that his life's work in the United States was finished, and that he was returning to his native land to die. Several prospective repatriates sought a change because of poor health, believing that the climate of Greece would aid them. Still others were journeying home to acquire wives and begin life anew. A young man, probably in his late twenties or early thirties, was on his way to marry a girl with whom he had corresponded but whom he had never met; he honestly believed, thanks to his parents' convincing talk, that a wife who had been born and raised in Greece, and had experienced hardship, was preferable to one born, raised, and pampered in the United States. An older man, possibly in his late fifties or early sixties, was just beginning another search for a mate; voluble and boastful, he expected to find the right woman, preferably a young one. The fact that he was advanced in years failed to curb his enthusiasm. To him the time element was not important, for he felt that he could afford to wait a year or two, if necessary. Some passengers claimed they were returning to Greece to relax; in the United States they had labored long and hard, and the time had come for them to lead a more leisurely life. A young medical student, born of immigrant parents in the United States, was on his way back to complete his final year of studies at the University of Athens. He, along with several others of Greek-American background, was attending the School of Medicine in Athens because he was unable to gain admission to an American medical school. Still another passenger bound for Greece, though planning only an indefinite stay, threatened to remain permanently if the Republicans won the election in 1952. He blamed the Republicans for the loss, in 1932, of most of the $32,000 he had deposited in the bank, and had been cursing them ever since. A kindly, elderly lady who

PREFACE

had come to America with the idea of residing with one of her sons conceded that the United States was a fine country for strong, young men, but felt that it was not the proper environment for people advanced in years, such as herself, who had spent most of their lives in Greece.

These shipboard conversations provided a valuable introduction to my research project, but the real answers to my inquiries, I knew, lay in Greece. Once there my problem again became twofold: to locate as many Greek-Americans as possible, and to ferret out all available sources of information in the libraries of Athens. The former task proved even easier than I had expected. I knew in advance of four convenient and readily accessible starting points: two confectionery stores in Athens, both operated by returned immigrants, one of whom I had heard about in my home town; the American Legion headquarters in Athens; and the various individuals employed by the Mutual Security Administration in different parts of Greece. In addition, the American Consul-General in Athens took a personal interest in my project from the outset, and many of the employees in his office also came forward with suggestions. Together these contacts furnished me with opportunities to meet as many returned Greek-Americans as I could hope to interview. After talking to them, recording their accounts, and rechecking their stories, I planned to seek out individuals whose basic experience differed from the general pattern that was evolving. After the first twenty or thirty interviews, I found this a far more challenging task than I had anticipated. The general experiences of many were similar, if the details were not.

It had always been my intention to travel into as many parts of Greece as possible, though occasionally my enthusiasm may have faltered because of Americans who had found the food and lodging outside Athens to their disliking. But as time elapsed, my determination to travel in the provinces grew. Well-founded rumor had it that Athens was unrepresentative of Greece; to meet Greeks, one had to visit the smaller cities and towns, even the villages. Accordingly I traveled far and wide—to Janina, near the Albanian border; to Arta, Agrinion,

PREFACE

Navpaktos, the modern site of historic Lepanto; to Volos, Larissa, and Salonika; to Corinth, Patras, Navplion, Tripolis, Megalopolis, Sparta, and to other smaller communities in the Peloponnesus and in Attica; and to the islands of Rhodes, Crete, Mytilene, Mykonos, and Hydra.

Whether in the greater Athens area, or in these scattered sections of Greece, the process of finding Greek-Americans proved intriguing. At the Athens airport, for example, on my way to the outlying provinces, I engaged in conversation with a Greek-American who had returned to Greece for the first time since his departure forty-one years before. A mild-appearing, soft-spoken man, he was on his way to visit the acquaintance who had welcomed him to the United States in 1912. The latter had returned to Greece to fight in the Balkan Wars in 1912–1913 and had remained in his native land.

It was simple to find Greek-Americans in the villages. Often a stop at the coffeehouse, or a brief conversation with a villager, was all that was necessary. The discovery of one repatriated immigrant led almost instantly to the "rounding up" of the rest. The one told the other.

Even in larger communities my task was not too difficult, for people in general were courteous and coöperative. In Patras, the largest city in the Peloponnesus, for instance, finding the first Greek-American was as easy as finding a police officer. Within ten minutes of registering at the Majestic Hotel, I asked the desk clerk if there were any Greek-Americans in the neighborhood. He directed me to the cigarette shop next door, whose owner was a repatriated immigrant. While we were chatting, a customer who also happened to be a Greek-American sauntered in, and told me an involved and pathetic story. After spending about an hour and a half with these two men, I returned to my hotel. No sooner had I stepped into my room than the telephone rang. When the desk clerk told me that another customer in the cigarette store was willing to talk to me, I immediately returned and began my interview with him.

Chance encounters frequently gave me the introductions I needed. While walking leisurely through a side street in Larissa,

PREFACE

the principal city of Thessaly, I spotted a copper shop and paused to inquire the prices of the articles on display. But the proprietor seemed to be just as interested in knowing who I was and where I came from as he was in selling his merchandise. Before long we were talking about the United States. Hardly had we started our conversation when the neighboring coffeehouse man with the inevitable tray came walking in. "Ah, here is another American," said the coppersmith. It required no coaching on my part to get the newcomer to talk about his American experiences. In keeping with Greek custom, he invited me to his shop for a cup of coffee, thus providing a pleasant social atmosphere for our conversation.

Chance again aided me in Mytilene, an island in the northeastern Aegean Sea. While I was sitting on a bench along the water front, I overheard two men engage in a conversation that caught my attention. One of the men spoke of having American dollars, and the other jestingly referred to the large quantities of olive oil he had to sell and the money he would receive. As they were about to go their separate ways, I heard such words as "Oh" and "John," and other expressions that confirmed my belief that the older of the two was a returned Greek-American. I went up to him and, rather apologetically, asked him if he had ever lived in the United States. "Yes," he replied. "I returned in 1951. I lived in Chicago Heights most of the thirty-eight years I spent in the United States. I came here to live on my social security pension."

Although, as the above illustrations indicate, I had little trouble in making contact with Greek-Americans, other phases of my research presented serious problems, problems that are likely to confront the contemporary historian in any field. The nature of my work required the use of the personal interview and the questionnaire. Both of these methods had their weaknesses, though there were of course compensating features. Sometimes I felt that the person interviewed sought to please by giving what he considered a "proper" instead of an honest answer. On one occasion a villager suspected me of being the representative of a government credit agency seeking informa-

PREFACE

tion about a debtor. More than once curious bystanders handicapped the questioning process by crowding around to hear what was said. Often I deemed it unwise to display the mimeographed questionnaire form I used, since it looked too official for some people. When this was true, I talked with the repatriate informally, trying to elicit replies to the questions with which I was familiar. After such an interview I jotted down the answers as quickly as possible.

My research problem was further complicated by the character of the people whom I interviewed. The returned immigrant was a subject charged with human emotions and contradictions. Nine successive years of fighting, to which many of the repatriated had been subjected, had aggravated the tendency toward instability. Moreover, returned immigrants were accorded different treatment in different places; in some areas they were ignored and almost forgotten, whereas in others they were singled out and respected. This variation made it difficult for me to evaluate my findings.

In general, the persons interviewed fell into three categories. First, there were the emotional, easily excitable Greek-Americans who tended to be dramatic in their answers and reactions; many of them expressed profound regret for having returned to Greece. Second, there were those who seemed more sincere, who spoke judiciously and calmly about their feelings for Greece; what they lacked in spontaneity and emotional fervor they made up for in a sense of responsibility. The third type of returned immigrant was the least satisfactory of all, for he concocted his answers on the spur of the moment in order to create the right impression. I met more of this kind of Greek-American than I cared to.

Admittedly questioning repatriates about events that had occurred twenty and thirty years before was not the most desirable way of obtaining reliable information. But because the available printed materials were exceedingly limited, as will be seen in the discussion of sources and bibliography, interviews were obviously the most important source for my research. And indeed they proved to be very revealing. Returned immigrants

PREFACE

often were persons advanced in years and willing to talk about their wealth of personal experiences. Postponement of the project until such time as library sources would be more informative would have aggravated instead of facilitated matters, for the death of many of the repatriates would have left the picture more incomplete than ever. It therefore seemed more sensible to utilize all the "live materials" at hand, and to trust that future scholars might some day capitalize on these preliminary findings and adduce new information to provide the fuller story that we would like.

My indebtedness to people who aided me at different stages of my research is great. Scores of Greeks and Greek-Americans narrated their experiences and observations to me; the list of their names is too lengthy to reproduce here. The staffs of the New York Public Library and of the libraries of the University of California, Los Angeles, the University of Chicago, Northwestern University, and Columbia University were most courteous.

Among those who aided me in Greece, I feel especially grateful to Mr. Stavros Skopeteas of the Library of the Greek Parliament and his aides, and to the personnel of the Benaki Library, the Gennadius Library, the National Library in Greece, the United States Educational Foundation in Greece, and the Near East Foundation in Athens. Mr. David C. Berger, United States Consul-General in Athens, and Mr. Print Hudson, the Agricultural Attaché, were consistently helpful. Mr. E. E. Wynne, Mr. John Asher, and other members of the Mutual Security Administration were unfailing in their courtesy and coöperation.

Special thanks must be extended to the Conference Board of Associated Research Councils for making it possible for me to obtain a Fulbright Research Award to Greece, without which this project would never have been completed; to the Research Committee of the University of California, Southern Section, which contributed funds for travel in the United States; and to the Social Science Research Council, which gave me the opportunity to take part in the seminar on cultural exchange.

PREFACE

The study would be incomplete without an expression of appreciation to Professors John D. Hicks and Oscar Handlin, Dean Theodore C. Blegen, and Mr. Glenn Gosling who read the manuscript at different stages, and whose suggestions in many instances were incorporated into the final draft. I am also indebted to Dr. Grace Stimson who saw the manuscript to press, and whose keen eye and penetrating criticisms saved me from a number of mistakes. However, I and I alone must be held responsible for any errors of fact or interpretation that may have crept into the study.

Theodore Saloutos

Los Angeles, California
September, 1955

CONTENTS

CHAPTER ONE
    AMERICA AND THE GREEK
    IMMIGRANT   1

CHAPTER TWO
    MOTIVES, ATTITUDES, AND STATUS
    OF THE REPATRIATED GREEK   29

CHAPTER THREE
    READJUSTMENT IN GREEK
    SOCIETY   57

CHAPTER FOUR
    ECONOMIC FORTUNES AND
    MISFORTUNES   74

CHAPTER FIVE
    SOME CASE HISTORIES   88

CHAPTER SIX
    THE REPATRIATED AND
    THEIR CRITICS   103

CHAPTER SEVEN
    SOME GREEK-AMERICAN
    INFLUENCES   117

APPENDIX   133

NOTES   135

SOURCES AND BIBLIOGRAPHY   143

INDEX   151

TABLES

1. IMMIGRANTS WHO DEPARTED FROM THE UNITED STATES, 1908–1931 — 30

2. COMPARISON, BY FISCAL YEAR, OF GREEK EMIGRANT ALIENS DEPARTED WITH EMIGRANT ALIENS DEPARTED WHO GAVE GREECE AS COUNTRY OF INTENDED FUTURE RESIDENCE, 1908–1952 — 52

3. OLD-AGE AND SURVIVORS' INSURANCE PAID TO RECIPIENTS LIVING ABROAD, 1940–1953 — 85

4. RAILROAD RETIREMENT AND SOCIAL SECURITY PAYMENTS IN GREECE, 1949–1952 — 85

5. PAYMENTS TO VETERANS OF THE FIRST WORLD WAR IN GREECE, 1949–1952 — 86

6. IMMIGRANT REMITTANCES RECEIVED IN GREECE, 1910–1950 — 120

CHAPTER ONE

AMERICA AND THE GREEK IMMIGRANT

IF ONE were asked to name the most conspicuous development in the immigration movement during the last decade of the nineteenth century, he would most assuredly point to the change in the national and geographic origins of most immigrants to the United States. What is more, he could elaborate by adding that this development marked the reversal of a trend deeply rooted in American history. No longer were the English, the Germans, the Irish, and the Scandinavians preponderant among the immigrants. In their places came the Italians, the Austro-Hungarians, the Russians, and others from southern and eastern Europe. This was truly the generation of the "new immigration."[1]

Among these so-called new immigrants were the Greeks, who were new in the literal meaning of the word. Only a few lived in this country before 1900, and the prospects of more arriving in the immediate future looked slim indeed. Except on rare occasions, Greek newspapers, periodicals, and publishing firms gave slight coverage to the New World. The professional classes had their ties with London, Vienna, Paris, Berlin, and other continental points. The United States, in their opinion, was one of those surviving outposts of civilization to which the poverty-stricken, the adventurers, the wealth-seekers, and the failures at home went to better their lot. It was also the land of the Irish,

---

[1] For notes to chap. 1, see pp. 139–141.

the Germans, the Italians, the Chinese, the Negroes, and other unassimilated religious and ethnic groups. Instead of selecting the United States, emigrating Greeks usually went to Egypt, Rumania, Russia, Turkey, Italy, and other European lands close to home. Except for the 8,515 who officially lived in the United States at the turn of the century, the Greeks had failed to discover the New World.

But once the Greeks began emigrating to the United States, hopefuls from all corners of the kingdom of Greece and from the "unredeemed parts" joined the movement. The Peloponnesians, coming from the oldest and perhaps the poorest section of the country, departed in sizable numbers. Specifically, the Laconians left first, and were followed by the Arcadians who eventually outnumbered them. The Laconians and the Arcadians were soon joined by villagers from Sterea Hellas, Thessaly, the Dodecanese, and Turkey in Europe, including the isles in the eastern Aegean Sea, and by the Greeks from Asia Minor.[2]

The reasons the Greeks left home to go to America after 1900, instead of before, are reasonably clear. The end of the short-lived war between Greece and Turkey in 1897 freed potential emigrants from military service, and meanwhile the United States had begun to work its way out of the depression of the mid-nineties. Simultaneously, the restlessness among the peasant classes of the Peloponnesus, caused by a series of crop failures, had opened the eyes of many to the possibilities offered by emigration to the United States.[3]

The most important reason for Greek emigration was "the monotonous, mournful, disheartening... cry of hunger." Greece was economically sick, and gave slight evidence of possessing the ability to recover. The country lacked natural resources and industries. The physical surface was covered by mountains, hills, boulders, and broken pieces of rock; most of the soil was untillable, and the methods of farming were primitive. The peasants barely eked out an existence from the marginal and submarginal lands they cultivated. Capital was scarce, and interest rates were as high as 10, 20, or 30 per cent. The certainty of a grim future forced many young people to look to the "unknown land" beyond the seas for opportunities their own country was unable to provide.⁴

By contrast the United States was the "Nation of Wealth." Nothing appealed to youth as much as stories of the riches awaiting those who had the courage to go after them. The prospect of returning home an enriched man within a brief time was a strong inducement. The sentiment in favor of emigration frequently crystallized in exhortations addressed to young people:

> Why remain here to struggle for a piece of bread without any security for the future, without honor and independence? Why not open your eyes and see the good that awaits you; harden your heart and seek your fortune abroad, where so many of your countrymen already have made theirs?
>
> Why linger? To protect your parents? Today or tomorrow, whether their children are here or abroad, they will close their eyes forever. It will be better for you to leave home and send a little money to provide for them in their advancing years.
>
> Or are you waiting to cultivate the barren lands with the ploughshare and dig in the fields? Have you seen how much progress you have made thus far?⁵

The economic image of the United States held by prospective immigrants varied. At first naïve villagers believed that the streets of America were paved with gold. But this illusion soon wore off. The less gullible dreamed of the emergence of some "Greek Astor and Vanderbilt and Rockefeller, a new Sinas and Zappas and Averoff and Syngros, who would provide employment in the United States...." Others expected to establish themselves in small businesses that eventually would make them independent.⁶

A Greek parliamentary committee, investigating immigration possibilities, graphically described the attraction of the United States for the depressed people of Europe and Asia: "It is the strength of a new nation, strong, energetic, drastic, tireless, making gigantic strides forward, building large cities, creating excellent opportunities, advancing civilization vigorously and happily. It is the strength [of a nation] with colossal capital in circulation, and capable of providing means of transportation on the ocean and into the interior which beckons the myriads of working hands.'" Truly it was youth calling to youth.

Steamship brokers and moneylenders enhanced the appeal of the New World by wide advertisement of its opportunities. Pictures of transatlantic liners, placed in village stores and coffeehouses, helped to give emigration a realistic touch. Representatives of shipping companies penetrated into remote areas, sounding the call to go to America. Often they spread false and irresponsible stories of the job and wealth opportunities awaiting the peasants. A moneylender, a former immigrant who had returned with savings, persuaded many to emigrate so that they too might share in his good fortune. A creditor usually offered to lend money at the prevailing high rate of interest and accept as security a mortgage on the property of a prospective emigrant. This business could be very lucrative. If a bad credit risk who had been encouraged to borrow was unable to keep up his payments, the lender could profit from the transaction by taking possession of the borrower's property.

The prospective immigrant was also preyed upon by the labor agent, whose unethical practices were all too common. The agent might promise the immigrant a job working with a relative or acquaintance of his, perhaps on a railroad construction gang in the United States, furnish him with a steamship ticket, and take a mortgage on his property. Even more vicious was the practice of lending money to the parents of a destitute youth for the latter's passage, and extracting from the father a promise that his son would work for a definite period of time. Security was usually demanded in such an arrangement.

Letters sent from America by friends or relatives often spoke optimistically of life in the United States, and sometimes contained the cost of passage. Such communications might have a contagious effect on an entire village, spreading the fever to pack up and leave for more promising shores. One immigrant wrote his former employer: "Here people work hard and regularly, and rest only on Sundays, but we fare well. Today, the day I write is Sunday. I have taken my bath, I have had my milk, and I will pass the day happily. When did I know life with such order in Greece? If you wish, master, you will do well to come, and I'll send you the cost of passage." Although stories of hardship, illness, and misery also circulated, they failed to dampen the enthusiasm of those who wanted to emigrate.[8]

Contrary to widespread Greek opinion, the courageous and resourceful rather than the helpless and hopeless members of rural society emigrated. Those who decided to leave were pessimistic about their economic prospects in Greece and optimistic about their future in America. Many of them were still in their twenties, with most of their lives ahead of them. Others were still younger—twelve, fifteen, seventeen, or nineteen years of age. Often youths left home at an age when American children were in grade school or just beginning high school. Such boys were fortunate if they had completed the village school, and rare indeed were those who had gone through the *gymnasion* (secondary school). In 1899 an emigrating party of fifty-two children, from a village near Sparta, left in quest of their fortune; most of the parents remained in Greece. A Macedonian, now residing in Salonika but once a resident of Buffalo, New York, told how he had helped to receive 120 boys from his home village, who arrived in the United States in 1908 on the steamship *Patris*, and how he had aided them in finding rooms and jobs. For such children parental affection and guidance were transmitted through correspondence, or postponed until they returned home.[9]

By 1910 the emigration of the young had reached alarming dimensions. It was estimated that from one-fifth to one-fourth of the total labor force of Greece had left for the United States. Military and government leaders were worried, for they could no longer dismiss the outflow as consisting only of the most undesirable elements in society. Greece was being drained of its most productive citizens and sapped of its potential military strength. This "national hemorrhage" had to cease if the country was to survive.[10]

The desire to escape military service was also a factor in the emigration movement. Greeks who took pride in their loyalty resented such charges and cited as evidence of patriotism the numbers who returned to fight in the Balkan Wars; but the testimony of some who came to the United States, and the unwillingness of many to return to fight as had been expected by the Greek authorities, proved that emigration was indeed an avenue of escape. A former immigrant, now a successfully established American businessman, admitted that his father had encouraged him to leave Greece to avoid serving in the army. He also said that other parents in his village had deliberately refrained from listing their sons with the census takers in order to keep their names out of the record books, and had likewise persuaded them to emigrate.

At first the Greek government made no attempt to prevent the departure of those in the military classes subject to call because it believed that the patriotism of its sons was inextinguishable, and that the pull of family ties and a strong nationalist psychology would insure their return. For a time it seemed that the assumptions of the government were well founded. In 1897, when war was declared against Turkey, several hundred emigrants returned home to fight, and others sent economic assistance from America. When the First Balkan War broke out in 1912, thousands returned to fight at their own expense. Truly the loyalty of these temporary expatriates seemed eternal, and the wisdom of the government's emigration policy appeared to be vindicated. But at the same time that these Greek nationals were coming home, thousands of others were preparing to avoid military service by emigrating. On the eve of the war in 1912 there were many who, aware of pending legislation to bar their exodus, hurriedly sold their crops in order to leave before the government could act.[11]

The fear that mass emigration would weaken home ties, and consequently lessen loyalty to Greece among the emigrants, aroused deep concern among some segments of the population. Nothing, from the standpoint of the tradition-bound, could be more reprehensible than a son's forsaking the Greek way of life, the hallowed customs and traditions of the village, and the treasured language of his ancestors. Although some people felt that this was inevitable, others minimized the danger by citing the earlier Greek emigrants who had made their fortunes abroad and had never forgotten their nationality. The more optimistic tried to reassure their skeptical compatriots by saying of the emigrants that "... they are Greeks and will remain Greeks.... Their paternal land will receive them again.... Emigrations such as these [are] but a continuation of the colonial movement of our ancestors ... who by living abroad temporarily enriched themselves, without at the same time diminishing their love for their country, and later as a result ... of their honorable labors abroad became the greatest providers and benefactors of the nation."[12]

Because of the widespread conviction that many Greeks who left for the United States would eventually return to their homeland, women played a minor role in the emigration movement. As a rule, the men expected to stay in America only long enough to make and save some money. But Greece soon became a nation with a surplus of women, weak, defenseless creatures in the literal sense of the world. As the heavy male outflow gradually widened the disparity, a number of courageous Greek women were induced to emigrate. Some of them, finding it difficult to attract husbands at home, hoped to capitalize on the shortage of their sex among Greeks in the United States. Others whose relatives at home could not provide them with dowries looked to the United States for matrimonial as well as economic salvation. Remarked one such immigrant: "I came to America in 1908 because my father was unable to provide me with a dowry. There were few Greek women in the country then and the men went begging for wives of their own nationality and religion."[13]

The emigration of large numbers of Greeks from 1904 to 1912 illustrated the pulsating effects of a national revival then sweeping the country. The spiritual, military, and political transformation that gripped the land was reflected in the stormy Macedonian events from 1904 to 1908, the Zorbas military reforms of 1909, and the mounting agitation of the Cretans for union with Greece. These developments assumed the proportions of a national renaissance; the invigorating impulse had seeped into the literary, cultural, and psychological realms. Greeks everywhere began to shake off the demoralizing thought that they were a shiftless, helpless, degenerate people beyond the hope of redemption. The emigrants, through the courage and determination they expressed, hoped to free themselves from the political and economic shackles that had bound them.[14]

Greeks residing in Ottoman Europe and in Asia Minor, similarly grown weary of poverty and intermittent war, also found emigration a welcome avenue of escape from undesirable conditions. The Greeks who left Turkey in Europe before 1911 were usually motivated by economic rather than military reasons. A Macedonian who emigrated to the United States in 1908 said, "I left Kastoria to escape from poverty more than to escape serving in the Turkish army." Another Macedonian added: "Turkey did not put pressure on the Greeks for service until 1911, when war against Italy broke out. Before this the Turks left the Greeks alone." A Greek-American who had spent many years in the United States and had returned in 1951 to Mytilene, an island in the northeastern Aegean Sea, stated: "I left in 1911 to escape serving in the Turkish army. A group of us, eight or nine, tried to leave once before, but we were caught and thrown in jail. After a brief imprisonment, we were given a ten-day leave and ordered to come back. I didn't go back as I was told. In those days people were leaving for the United States in droves. It was illegal to do this, but if you had money you could hire someone to row you out under darkness to some ship that was waiting to take those who wanted to leave. Then a gold sovereign or two was enough to do the job. It was easy to fool the Turks. . . ." Another repatriate who had been in the United States from 1911 to 1920 said, "I deserted from the Turkish army and came to America because I didn't want to kill Greeks."

Greeks also emigrated from Ottoman-occupied territory because they feared reprisals at the hands of the enemy. After the unfortunate war with Turkey in 1897, some Macedonians who had fought on the Greek side left for the United States instead of returning to their homes and risking punishment. Shortly before 1912, when a major conflict involving Greece, Bulgaria, and Turkey appeared imminent, many fled into Greece to remain permanently, or else to embark for the United States.[15]

The exact number of Greeks who came to America will probably never be known. The failure of the Greek government to keep accurate records, and the difficulty of clearly defining "a Greek," account for most of the confusion. The Greek definition of a Greek was more all-embracing than the American. The Greeks held that a person always retained his nationality. If his father was a Greek, he was also a Greek regardless of where he was born or where he lived. A middle-aged woman born in Constantinople observed that she had always considered herself a Greek even though she was born in Turkey and had spent many years there. She failed to understand why a person born of immigrant parents in the United States should regard himself as an American. A young Greek police officer likewise found it impossible to accept the idea that one born of a Greek father abroad was anything but a Greek. "Greek blood flows in your veins. You can't renounce it." American authorities, on the contrary, accepted the country of a person's birth as the determining factor in establishing nationality. The picture was further confused because the Greeks counted as their own many persons whom the Americans regarded as nationals of Turkey, Italy, and Rumania.

These conflicting standards produced conflicting estimates. Because the Greek definition of a Greek was broader than the American, the Greek figures for the number who entered the United States were substantially larger than the figures released by the American immigration authorities. *Atlantis*, the leading Greek-American daily, divided the immigrants into two categories: those from "free" Greece and those from "enslaved" Greece. On June 30, 1908, the newspaper estimated that about 150,000 of the former and 75,000 of the latter were residing in the United States. Immigrants from enslaved Greece included those who came from Turkey in Europe and Asia Minor, the islands in the Aegean Sea, and Rumania and Bulgaria. Another 25,000 were believed to have arrived in America from Crete,

Egypt, Cyprus, and nearby places. A Greek parliamentary committee, appointed to study immigration, placed the number who went to the United States between 1899 and 1911 at 253,983. Of this total, 199,055 came from free Greece and 54,928 from Turkey in Europe, Asia Minor, and other parts. It is likely that the committee obtained many of its data from American sources. In such calculations provision also had to be made for the numerous immigrants who entered the country illegally. Among these, sailors who deserted their ships when they reached port were predominant, although others were also known to have smuggled themselves into the country.[16]

Whether they came from Greece or from other countries, whether they were leaving home for economic or military reasons, the Greeks who emigrated to the United States fully realized the extent of their undertaking from the moment they obtained passage. They were indeed setting their faces toward the unknown. Those who were fortunate escaped the clutches of the usurer and of the unscrupulous ticket agent, and found themselves on board one of the vessels of the Austro-Americana Line, the National Steamship Company, the Fabre Line, or some other concern, traveling as steerage or third-class passengers. One writer aboard a transoceanic liner observed: "Many of them [emigrants] left their village for the first time and for the first time had seen the ocean which terrified them even when it was calm. They were melancholy and sat in small groups and spoke slowly. Every one of them must have been thinking of the village he left behind, his wife, his children, his parents...."
If fate was unkind the voyagers might experience one of those dreadful storms that made them curse Columbus for having discovered America. It seems incredible that people whose principal occupation in life had been herding goats and sheep, who had never been far from home before, and had no previous knowledge of the language, customs, and traditions of the United States, were heading for this distant land each with as little as fifteen or twenty dollars in his pocket.[17]

Many thoughts passed through the mind of the emigrant as he crossed the Atlantic, but one of the most frightening was the possibility of being rejected by the immigration authorities and compelled to return to Greece empty-handed. "For one to be accepted in the Paradise of America, he had to pass through the Purgatory of Ellis Island." As his ship approached American waters, the prospective immigrant heard tales of those who had been accepted or rejected. One arrival said that the passengers aboard his ship were divided into two broad classifications: those who traveled in first or second class, and "the rest." For the first two classes, inspection was nominal at best; but the rest—those who had suffered day in and day out in the hold, or on the deck of the ship—had "to undergo a sort of 'Holy Confession' before they passed into the threshold of the New World."[18]

Once the immigrant had passed inspection at Ellis Island—"the island of hope and agony"—he usually headed for the home of a brother, a cousin, an uncle, or a village acquaintance. Because this was so, the geographic and occupational distribution of immigrants depended in some degree on where earlier immigrants lived and worked. The first arrivals tended to influence those who came later from the same village. During the early years it was common to find an unusually large number from a certain village employed on a particular railroad construction gang, or a disproportionately large group from the island of Karpathos, in the Dodecanese group, living in Tarpon Springs, Florida, and working as sponge divers. Although the old-world occupational background of the immigrant might have helped to determine his early employment and residence, he was more often decisively influenced by the location and work of the earlier arrival.

Despite the rural background of the overwhelming majority, the immigrants concentrated in urban areas. In 1900 at least half of the 8,515 Greeks officially in the United States lived in Chicago, Boston, Lowell, Philadelphia, San Francisco, and Savannah. As more and more Greeks arrived, they began fanning out in all directions. Soon Chicago, New York, Lowell, Detroit, and San Francisco had the largest Greek populations in the country. Lowell had an unusually large number for a city of its size.[19]

Some Americans condemned the newcomers for congregating in the cities instead of becoming small independent farmers. Such critics overlooked certain elementary facts. Granted that the choicer lands had been appropriated by the earlier immigrants, the railroads, corporations, and speculators, and that only the less desirable were available, the immigrant still associated farming with poverty, small crops, and futility. He wanted to turn his back on these unhappy memories. Furthermore, agriculture in the United States was conducted on a capitalistic basis, and the funds of the immigrant were few. Had he possessed the money needed to farm in the United States, he would probably never have left Greece. The immigrant lived a hand-to-mouth existence. He needed cash and he needed it quickly in order to provide for himself, for his anxious parents, or for the family he had left behind. Time and ready money were of the essence. Urban employment and street vending, not farming, offered the best opportunities to obtain ready cash. Certainly at first, when the immigrant came "to grab a few riches and hurry home," the thought of engaging in a long-range operation such as farming hardly entered his mind. Cash, mobility, and the dream of going home at the earliest opportunity dominated his thoughts.[20]

Moreover, the social aspects of farming in the United States frightened the immigrant. The American farmer lived in comparative isolation, not in a village consisting of close relatives and friends he had known for years. Farm life might drive the average Greek, who was a gregarious person, into insanity. He wanted to be with his countrymen who spoke the same language, celebrated the same holidays, and observed the same traditions. Few realized how lonely and uncomfortable the immigrant felt in his non-Greek surroundings. He craved the company of his compatriots. Should illness strike, he could count on their aid and sympathy or, as the village saying had it, "He had someone around who could hand him a glass of water when he needed it."[21]

In the cities, the occupations of the immigrants varied. Many, perhaps most, of the Greeks worked at one time or another in a restaurant or a confectionery store, either as employees or proprietors, or possibly as both. Railroad construction work, fruit and flower peddling were common. Shoe shining, hat cleaning, and pants pressing were occupations that attracted Greeks. One repatriated Greek-American, currently a prominent steamship ticket broker in Athens, said that during his three years in the United States he had worked in a restaurant, served as a water boy on a railroad construction gang, and had been employed in a candy store, a biscuit factory, a shoe factory, and a St. Louis carshop. Another, a contented peasant in a Peloponnesian village, stated: "I was a bootblack for two years. I sold fruit. Then I opened a lunchroom and restaurant. I owned a place in Montgomery, Alabama, that employed eighteen people." Still another, now the successful head of a travel agency, remarked, "I was in the restaurant business the six years I was in the United States. I began as a waiter, then became a cashier, and the third year a partner." A Greek-American originally from Asia Minor, now a resident of Athens, had worked as an elevator man, an electrician, and a chef. One of the most prosperous repatriates in Greece had been in the ice-cream business with his brothers in Chicago. A former restaurant man described his economic fortunes as follows: "I began as a bus boy, then became a chef and pastry cook. I had my own restaurant. One summer I bought, reorganized, and resold at a profit thirteen restaurants."

The immigrants launched other enterprises and did other kinds of work, too. They managed laundries, bottling plants, fur shops, coffeehouses, barber shops, and saloons. Some worked in steel foundries and tin factories. A few painted houses and dove for sponges. One immigrant became a part-time puppeteer. Several went to college and obtained degrees in dentistry and engineering. A young man who had lived in the United States twelve years spent four of them in high school, four in college, and four in the ranks of the unemployed. One of the most novel pursuits was that of a former laborer who became a successful gambler and bootlegger.[22]

There were few intellectuals and professional people among

AMERICA AND THE GREEK IMMIGRANT

Greek immigrants. "... A cultured Greek, like a cultured immigrant from any nationality, [was] at no advantage.... However cultivated [he might have been], however gifted in rhetoric, however exact in his use of the 'written Greek,' he was doomed to disappointment and failure without the cruder virtues of the peasant. America ask[ed] of its immigrants not firmness but strength." And strength was precisely what the typical Greek immigrant was prepared to offer.[23]

Even if the Greek immigrant found congenial employment, and was fortunate enough to live among friends or relatives from his homeland, his path was not easy. The difficulties of adjustment during the early years were numerous, almost overpowering, and left the newcomer with lasting and not too happy impressions of the United States. And so many problems appeared simultaneously; they didn't wait their turns. All at once, it seemed, the immigrant had to learn a new language, protect himself from an unscrupulous countryman (the so-called interpreter), adjust to the discipline of an industrial society, become acquainted with the customs and traditions of the land, overcome homesickness, endure nativist opposition, and acclimate himself to a society composed of diverse ethnic and religious groups.

Because the English language was radically different from Greek, the immigrant required time to learn it. "I ask you," pleaded one youth, "how can I learn English when I don't even know Greek?" The language problem made it difficult for the newcomer to communicate with his employer, or immediate overseer. In handling personal affairs he relied on an interpreter of his own nationality, described as one who knew "thirty or forty words in English," often less, and who furnished his linguistic talents to his less versatile compatriots for a good price. Frequently, the interpreter was a "shyster" who, pretending to know some law, subjected his victims to the most incredible frauds. On shopping expeditions the immigrant who spoke no English had to use gestures, even pantomime, to make his wants known to the clerk. Inability to read English also brought him into conflict with the law. In 1895 about 100 Greeks were fined weekly in New York City, and about forty in Boston, for violating municipal ordinances of one kind or another.[24]

The opportunities for exploiting the immigrant were seemingly limitless. Often the expatriated Greek had more to fear from his own countrymen than from his new neighbors. In some instances the exploitation began before he left Greece and continued for months, or perhaps for a year or two, after he reached the United States, depending on the contractual arrangement he had made with the person who advanced him the cost of passage.

A frequently cited case was that of a pseudo labor agent who recruited workers for his brother in Kansas City. "Go to my brother who will give you work at a dollar sixty-five a day on the railroad he manages," was his advice to three innocent prospects. "But we don't have the money to pay for our passage," replied the three. "I will provide you with tickets," answered the agent, "which cost five hundred and fifty drachmas each, if each of you turn your lands over to me as security, and I will send you [to the United States] with a warranty, so that you will not be rejected by the authorities, because I have arranged with the transoceanic ship that will take you to New Orleans and not New York; I shall also guarantee you work with my brother at a dollar sixty-five a day, and I am sure that in two or three months you will be able to pay your debt. You can pay the money to my brother in Kansas, it is the same."

The three peasants, deciding to emigrate, drew up contracts containing these terms in Corinth. They gave their property as security for 550 drachmas, which they said they received in cash. This, of course, was a falsehood. Three days later they left for Patras with the agent, who gave each one a prepaid ticket on the Austro-Americana Line. The emigrants were advised to tell the American authorities that they had paid for their own passage, and that they were not sure what kind of work they were going to do in the United States.

The three reached Kansas City and were given the promised jobs, but were laid off after working for thirteen days. When they received their wages, they discovered that $5.50 had been deducted from each pay envelope as a "duty," and another 50 cents to purchase a suit of clothes for the "director of the line." From then on, they lived on false hopes and promises, for their jobs had ended. When one of the three immigrants complained to the Greek authorities about the swindle, he learned that the passage from Patras to New Orleans cost only 255 drachmas; through ignorance he had agreed to pay 550 drachmas and to give his lands as security for an amount he never received. These two brothers brought about eighty others to the United States under the same arrangement.[25]

But even more vicious practices were identified with the *padrone* system, a twentieth-century version of the system that brought indentured servants to America during the seventeenth century. The *padrone* system gave immigrants a very unfavorable impression of life in the United States. Bootblacks, construction gang workers, and fruit and vegetable peddlers in particular were its victims during the early years; many employing Greeks made rapid headway in the shoe-shining business because they were able to recruit cheap labor in this way.

The system operated in this fashion. A recruiter of labor got in touch with the parents of a youth who wanted to come to America, but who lacked the means of transportation. The father and the agent connived to break the law because they believed the transaction would be mutually advantageous; the parent would get his son to America, and the agent would receive a commission. The youth, anywhere from fifteen to nineteen years of age, was promised a job. If underage, he was accompanied by a "false-father," an adult who posed as a father to get the boy through inspection but then left him to travel the rest of the way alone.[26] The immigrant youth received free transportation to the United States and, after reaching his destination, a job, room and board, and a small monthly wage. A Greek-American who had experienced this ordeal revealed that as a youth he had been paid four dollars a month and had been fed on a steady diet of bean soup and bananas. Bootblacks were compelled either to hand their "tips" over to the "boss," or else to share them on a percentage basis determined arbitrarily by the employer. The profits of the *padrone* averaged from $100 to $200 annually for each boy employed and, under favorable circumstances, might reach $300 to $500 per boy. Cruel as the system was, a victimized parent often considered it a heaven-sent way of getting his son to America to harvest some of its riches.

The bootblack's workday was long—twelve, thirteen, or fourteen hours. The boys often had to work on Saturdays, Sundays, and holidays; in fact, the workday might be longer over the week end and on holidays, and the work more exacting and continuous, than during the week. Child labor laws were ignored. These youths, denied parental affection, toiling long hours, using ill-smelling dyes and polishes, bending over much of the time, eating inferior food, and working under unsanitary conditions, were destined almost inevitably to suffer deterioration of health and morals. For the victims of the *padrone* system there was no "free" America, at least for the time being.[27]

Employees in steel mills, mines, tanneries, and other plants, and workers on construction gangs found it equally difficult to adapt themselves to the discipline of an industrial society. The American workday, devoid of the afternoon rest period to which the Greek, along with other Europeans, had grown accustomed, was long and backbreaking. "From house to mill and from mill to house" was the daily routine, as described by one immigrant. The simple, casual life of working in the fields among friends and relatives was a thing of the past. Now the Greek-American had to rise in the morning at a regular hour, be at work at a regular hour, eat at a regular hour, and go home at a regular hour. The village coffeehouse, the square, and the holidays all were memories. "It was worse than being a horse hitched to a wagon."[28]

The small shopkeeper, though more fortunate than the laborer in some respects, and certainly more independent, also found his work hard and his hours long. Twelve, fourteen, sixteen, or even eighteen hours of work a day were common among the proprietary class. Sometimes this self-imposed routine was a matter of necessity. Earnings depended on whether the shopkeeper did the work himself or hired someone else to do it. A restaurant man, a confectioner, or a grocer saw potential savings diminished and his return to Greece delayed with every hired hand he employed. A Greek restaurant operator succeeded where another failed because he worked harder and longer. Thus the small businessman's exacting conditions were self-inflicted, but his better sense of business cautioned him against placing too much faith in an employee, or in a hired manager. "If you want your place in order, you have to be there yourself. Your help will rob you, if you aren't."[29]

The American diet caused the immigrant considerable trouble in the beginning. The cuisine was strange, the food almost unpalatable to him. Restaurants were later established to prepare the semioriental dishes to which he was accustomed.[30]

Often a group of six or eight men would rent a house, furnish it, and begin housekeeping on a coöperative basis. Each took his turn at cooking, washing, and cleaning house. An immigrant writer described one such venture as follows:

Our group consisted of three Cretans, one from Naxos [an island], two Messenians, two Cypriotes, and a Thessalian. Our furniture was made up of a table, ten chairs, a stove, two pitchers, a frying pan, a large dish, a combination ladle and fork, a *Beginners Method in English*, a dream book, and a picture of Paul Melas [a Greek hero].

Once we arranged our affairs, we chose Kyriakos as "boss" of the house. Kyriakos had been in the city for a year, knew about forty words in English, received the enviable salary of $8 a week, and had $200 in the bank which made him a man of means in those days.

As "boss" of the house Kyriakos had autocratic powers and he exercised them austerely in matters of food and expenses.... Kyriakos' permanent menu for the house was this:

Monday: Rice and wieners
Tuesday: Potatoes and wieners
Wednesday: Eggs and wieners
Thursday: Lentils and wieners
Friday: Greens and wieners
Saturday: Beans in cottonseed oil
Sunday: Meat, soup, and beer

The immigrant was also overwhelmed by the diverse national and religious origins of the people he met. It was confusing to find himself among people who spoke various languages and who worshiped in different churches. For the first time in his life he came into contact with a Pole, a German, a Frenchman, a Hungarian, a Slovak, a Russian, a Chinese, a Negro, or a representative of some other nationality group. Small wonder that one Greek humorously remarked: "We have been in America for six months.... We had neither heard English nor become acquainted with Americans. In the mill there worked Polish men and Polish women and only Polish was spoken in the factory and in the streets of the small town." And his friend added: "I believe the captain of our ship made a mistake and instead of bringing us to America brought us to Poland." A third, of more cosmopolitan bearing since he had spent two weeks in New York City, suggested that the others also go there "to see Americans and hear all the English [they] wanted."[31]

Often the immigrant felt unwanted. Of southern European origin and a late comer, he believed that representatives of the older immigrant groups resented his presence and that they inflicted on him the same kind of animosity visited upon them when they first arrived. Many of the Greeks remembered a time when they could not walk out of their quarters without being "tomatoed" or otherwise assaulted by "unbridled" youngsters, and subjected to the profanity of the parents. As an unskilled laborer and a foreigner too, the immigrant had slight chance of joining the American Federation of Labor whose policy had been anti-immigrant from the very beginning.[32]

Since the immigrant could read very little beyond the Greek language press and the headlines in American newspapers, his integration into American life was slow and painful. Unfamiliarity with the language and bewilderment caused by differences in customs and traditions bred a sense of insecurity, which in turn led to rationalization and an overidealization of Greece. Although the immigrant was fortunate if he possessed the bare rudiments of an elementary education, still he proudly associated himself with his illustrious Greek ancestors. There was something comforting and reassuring in this. He never forgot that his birthplace was also that of the ancients. By contrast, he felt that the United States was deficient in philosophy, literature, and fine arts. Its greatness rested on technological might, wealth, and material strength. Compared to the immigrant's own land, with its rich cultural background, America was boorish and unsophisticated. One immigrant remarked that even the dollar which gave the United States its prestige suffered from inflation.[33]

The immigrant's discontent with various phases of American life, plus his peasant background, tended to perpetuate ties with the homeland. His family and ancestors were rooted to the soil and bound by customs that had been handed down for generations. These were stabilizing influences, but they discouraged deviations from customary behavior patterns. Since all members of the family worked together to cultivate the lands and raise the farm animals, they were all entitled to a share in the meager earnings. Beyond the family was the village which also helped to cast the peasant's mold. As a rule, the individual did little independent thinking.

When the immigrant reached the United States, he found himself cut adrift from his stratified rural environment, from the family and village traditions he knew. Without the influences that had formerly governed his life, he found it enormously difficult to adjust to his new surroundings. The immigrant often felt lost or stranded, and was unable to cope with social and economic codes that were so sharply at variance with his familiar way of life. Fears of social annihilation forced him to seek the company of his compatriots. His peasant background, and the thousands of miles that separated him from home, guaranteed that he would cling tenaciously to the customs and traditions he had been taught to prize.[34] In the larger cities this feeling of insecurity, coupled with the desire to be near his place of employment or his business, the church, and those who spoke the same language and observed the same traditions, forced the immigrant to live in a Greek colony. Cheap rents and the inability to find better housing also tended in the same direction. But in outlying districts, the smaller cities and towns, the presence of a few Greeks, or even of only one or two, sharpened the immigrant's loneliness. Through his grinding hours of work and his anxieties, in the complete absence of family life, he hopefully awaited those better days he had always dreamed about. Small wonder that a Greek who traveled through a community, even though he might be a complete stranger, was welcomed by the sole Greek restaurateur or confectioner in town as though he were a long lost brother. The nationality bond between the transient and the resident was a comforting one.[85]

The Greeks, like other national groups, brought with them institutions they had known at home. They introduced the Greek Orthodox Church with its national and religious holidays, the parochial school or the Greek-American version of it, the local society, and the coffeehouse. The success of these institutions depended on their ability to adapt themselves to the needs of the immigrant, and on the intensity of the old-world loyalties of their constituents.

The Greek Orthodox Church, the most influential of the old-world institutions, figured prominently in immigrant life. The parish church became a fixture wherever a hundred or more immigrants settled. At first, many communities encountered difficulties in finding priests to minister to their spiritual needs. Until recent years, all priests were born, raised, and educated in Greece, or in the unredeemed parts, which naturally gave them an intensely pro-Greek outlook. This was emotionally satisfying to the immigrant because the Church was a constant reminder of his village, and even brought into the fold those who had been wayward members in Greece. During the Christmas and Easter seasons, many Greek-Americans who lived in suburban and outlying rural areas came to the metropolitan communities to attend church services. Even the "shoeshine parlor boss," who believed in working his helpers twelve and fifteen hours a day, made an exception during religious holidays, and the employee, who often labored long hours to increase his savings and facilitate his return home, compromised with his pocketbook in order to observe church festivals. During the earlier years particularly immigrants made determined attempts to celebrate name days and religious and patriotic holidays with the same fervor as in their old-world villages. But the immigrant soon discovered that there were too many obstacles to overcome. In the United States Church and state were separated. His new home was a land of opportunity, ceaseless toil, and limited hours of relaxation. There was much to do. Employment, and vastly different social conditions, militated against the observance of holidays with the same festive spirit known in Greece.

The priest reminded his parishioners that only through the faith and language of their parents could they maintain their national identity. Church leaders warned the immigrants against succumbing to the teachings of Protestants and non-canonical priests who were capitalizing on their spiritual needs, often misleading and seducing them into acceptance of strange and idolatrous creeds. Emphasis was placed on establishing Greek schools where young people would be instructed in the traditional faith and language. Endless warnings were issued against mixed marriages and deviations from the parental path. A real Greek was true to his religion and to the country of his birth.

For some years parish churches were the scenes of incessant rows between rival factions which struggled to control Church property and influence community policies. One riot in Chicago was of serious enough proportions to attract public attention. The scandalous situation arose when the defeated group refused to yield to the victorious faction the church records, the keys to the church building, and the paraphernalia needed to administer the church. Episodes of this type plagued one community after another. Appeals from conscientious Greeks to save their nationality from public disgrace often ended in failure, as one group after another took or threatened to take its case to the courts of law.

Shortly before, during, and after the First World War, old-world political disputes had even more violent repercussions than religious arguments on the churches throughout the United States. Two uncompromising and unyielding factions arose in most large communities. One faction supported the policies of King Constantine; the other endorsed the program of Eleutherios Venizelos, the liberal, pro-Ally spokesman from Crete. As a rule, Greeks from the Peloponnesus were royalists, and those from the islands, the unredeemed parts, and the newly annexed territories were Venizelists. Greek after Greek threw himself into the controversy with a vengeance, and for a time many of them were more concerned about the policies of Venizelos or of the King than they were about the domestic and foreign policies of the United States. In time royalist churches appeared to minister to communicants who believed in the policies of the King, while others catered to the spiritual needs of Venizelos sympathizers. Although the Greek-American press was widely criticized for perpetrating these bitter quarrels in the United States, Church leaders could hardly escape their share of the responsibility. The hierarchy was involved in the political dispute from the very outset, and helped to foster a factious spirit that divided one church community after another.[36]

Another popular old-world institution, of less exalted stature than the Church, was the coffeehouse. Exclusively male in its patronage, it served as a community center after working hours. It appeared wherever a sufficiently large number of Greeks settled in one locality. Little capital was required to establish a coffeehouse. A large enough hall or store was rented and filled with tables and chairs. With a few pounds of coffee, several narghiles, some playing cards and slates to keep score, the aproned proprietor, his shoulder draped with the inevitable cleaning towel, was in business. In the kitchen he brewed the coffee he served to his customers with "lokum," "baklava," or other Oriental delicacies. He also dispensed bottled American soft drinks, and sometimes drinks that were not soft. On the walls one was likely to see framed lithograph pictures of a Greek revolutionary hero, of a battle in which the Greek emerged the victor and the Turk the loser, or of a Greek strong man. There might also be displayed announcements of a forthcoming community event, a death, or a memorial service, the picture of an old-world political favorite of the proprietor and his clients—in a royalist coffeehouse, for example, one never saw the portrait of Venizelos—and the array of advertisements found in any popular meeting place.[37]

Despite the criticisms leveled against it, the coffeehouse was a remarkably democratic institution in which people from all walks of life gathered to play cards, sip a cup of thick, black Turkish coffee, lazily draw on a narghile, or indulge in an animated discussion of politics. The atmosphere of the coffeehouse, clouded with foul cigarette or cigar smoke, was hardly inviting to the public eye or nose. But this was the place to hear local gossip, who died or who was getting married, who was leaving for Greece or who was returning to America; to exchange information, or misinformation, on the latest trend in employment, the competence or incompetence of the teacher, the priest, the president of this or that society; and to discuss and perhaps appraise the children of the various members of the community.[38]

A coffeehouse often featured gambling games which were popular with those patrons who sought to escape from their humdrum existence. According to numerous newspaper accounts, police raids were a common occurrence during the early years. Coffeehouse proprietors often agreed to permit gambling because it was profitable. In Los Angeles a Republican Political Club, formed for the ostensible purpose of conducting political discussions, served as a blind for gambling.[39]

Impromptu political discussions always played a part in the social gatherings in the coffeehouse. Old-world politics came in for close scrutiny. Observers unfamiliar with the Greek language and arguing techniques might easily have mistaken these discussions for bitter quarrels. But the conflicts were merely verbal, and only tables or chairs suffered blows from the excitable participants. The Greeks, like other Europeans, accompanied "their words with multiple gestures of hands and head, maybe even the foot, or the whole body."[40]

The coffeehouse also served as a place of amusement. In

larger communities there might be a semioriental floor show, staged by women of questionable talent and virtue. Less pretentious *Karagiozi* or silhouette shows were produced by a clever performer who, working alone, demonstrated a capacity for changing his voice and for gesticulating to denote a change in characters. In such spectacles a Greek always appeared as the hero and a Turk as the villain, though an enterprising artist displaying his talents in a Turkish settlement might reverse the order. These exhibitions were usually interspersed with intermissions so that the performer could regain his breath and also pass the tray for contributions, which might be augmented or diminished in accordance with his card-playing fortunes after the show. Well-fed strong men, such as steel- and iron-twisters, lifters of water-filled barrels, and other stunt performers, exhibited their acts before open-mouthed but appreciative spectators who were delighted to see that the Herculean strength of the Greeks was a thing of the present as well as of the past."[1]

Next to the coffeehouse, the community organization and the local society furnished the setting for social functions of various types. In addition to their usual meetings, the members enjoyed periodic native dances and annual picnics, and occasionally staged amateur plays. At first the local benefit society was the most prominent; as early as 1908 there were about three hundred of them in existence. Organized on the basis of the village, the eparchy, the province, or the island from which the members came, a benefit society took the name of a patron saint, a local revolutionary hero, or someone who was in some way identified with the locality. The society usually provided medical and social benefits for the members, who paid a stipulated monthly fee. Unfortunately, the mortality rate of this kind of organization was high. Dissatisfaction with the physician hired by the society, arbitrariness on the part of the officials, unreasonable demands made by some of the members, and the frequent quarrels that sometimes assumed community proportions helped to seal their fate.

Later on, regional and national organizations were formed. Among the regional groups were the Pan-Arcadian, the Pan-

Laconian, the Pan-Messenian, the Pan-Cretan, and the Pan-Icarian societies. At least three major national organizations appeared: the Panhellenic Union; the American Hellenic Educational Progessive Association (AHEPA); and the Greek American Progressive Association (GAPA). The first of the three was a pre-World War I organization, whereas the latter two came into being during the nineteen-twenties and reflected the cleavages that cut through various communities across the country.⁴²

Wrestling and boxing matches attracted some interest, especially when one of the participants was a Greek. In the early years the names of "Jeem" Londos, Bill Demetral, "Jeemy" Demetral, John Kilonis, and other less well-known performers were bywords among compatriots, who often crowded into the ringside seats to encourage their countryman to "break the bone" of his opponent.⁴³

In addition to all these forces working to preserve the national identity of the immigrants, there were still other agencies directed to the same end. Prominent Greek leaders believed that their American compatriots had to play the same positive role in nationalist affairs as did the earlier emigrants to Russia, England, Austria, Egypt, Rumania, and other lands. It made little difference if a Greek had lived abroad for many years, had become a citizen of a foreign country, or had attained a high government post in another land; he was still expected to be loyal to the home of his fathers. It was for such reasons that the names of Capodistria, Benaki, Zappas, Arsakis, Syngros, and various others were honored. They had lived abroad and had won fame and fortune there, but had never forgotten that they were Greeks. Much the same kind of patriotism was expected of those residing in the United States. If need be, they were supposed to come to the support of Greece with their blood or money, perhaps with both.⁴⁴

The Greek language press did more than its share in helping the immigrant maintain his interest in his birthplace, even though the editors sometimes appeared to be pursuing a vacillating and opportunistic course. During the earler years, much if not most of the news carried by the Greek-American press was foreign, but with the passage of time the amount of domestic news increased. Besides printing accounts of Greek happenings, the press also kept in close touch with local community affairs; for many it served as a sort of daily classroom in preserving and cultivating the native language. It published news of old-world feuds and helped to generate new ones of a local character. It carried accounts of Bulgarian atrocities in Macedonia, the movement for Cretan independence, Greek irredentist claims, military reforms, the Balkan Wars, and the activities of Greek enemy agents in the United States.[45]

The first and most influential of the Greek dailies was *Atlantis*, founded in 1894 in New York and destined to become a vital force in the lives of Greek-Americans. Its publisher was Solon J. Vlastos, a shrewd and successful newspaperman who acquired a following before establishing his paper by catering to the immediate interests of the immigrants. His dynamic, competitive spirit led him into many battles with subordinates, business rivals, and personal antagonists. Among Vlastos' first major encounters was a fight with the ill-fated *Panhellenios*, the organ of bitter personal rivals who pooled their resources to break his alleged "newspaper monopoly" over the Greek-Americans. Vlastos, emerging victorious from the clash with *Panhellenios*, then engaged in his most important battle, a long conflict with the *National Herald*. This paper was founded for the specific purpose of combating the royalist sympathies of *Atlantis* and presenting the Venizelos argument to Greek-Americans. For years these two dailies engaged in fierce journalistic battles that rocked one Greek community after another, shamefully divided church congregations, and often destroyed business partnerships and social friendships.[46]

If there was something comforting in having a Greek newspaper to read, a Greek Orthodox church to attend, a coffeehouse to frequent, or a society to join, there were other aspects of life that tended to make the immigrant restless. Sometimes the immigrant revealed his discontent in complaints about his empty, monotonous, unrelaxed life, or in frequent trips between the

United States and Greece. Although such voyages might have been prompted by business needs, they also reflected restlessness. One Greek-American made about thirty crossings. Another required eighteen ocean journeys, or nine round trips, before he could decide where to live permanently. Many others made three, four, or five round trips.

This was the America of the Greek-American. The United States was "the land of the goose that laid the golden egg," "the full mouth," "milk and honey," and "everything that is good." Here a man could labor, save, be spared from military duty, and associate with whomever he pleased. He could exercise his individual rights, as long as he did not interfere with those of others. But America was also a land of ceaseless toil, of different customs and traditions, of people who thought and behaved differently. Nostalgic memories of home often made the immigrant yearn for what he had left behind.

CHAPTER TWO

MOTIVES, ATTITUDES, AND STATUS OF THE
REPATRIATED GREEK

THE GREEKS were but one of many immigrant groups to repatriate themselves. From 1908 to 1931 inclusive a total of 4,077,263 representatives of all nationalities left the United States, presumably to return to their native lands to live. A statistical breakdown (see table 1) shows that the Greeks ranked fourth among the first ten immigrant groups whose members returned home in substantial numbers. Of the more than half a million Greeks admitted into the United States by 1931, roughly 40 per cent, or 197,000, went back to their homeland.

Among the repatriates were many who were simply fulfilling their original intention of returning home as soon as their economic status permitted. But these, as well as immigrants who had never contemplated a return journey, were impelled by differing reasons to leave the United States. Motives varied from person to person, from period to period. Ofter a single motive, but a combination of circumstances, contributed to an immigrant's decision to go home. In seeking to discover such motives and circumstances, I found that the repatriate himself sometimes tried to conceal the real reasons for his action. But what one was reluctant to reveal, another was willing to disclose; if the repatriate hesitated to give a full explanation, a son, or a wife, or a brother might embellish the story he told.

There is no doubt that some repatriates were influenced by

the spasmodic efforts of prominent Greek individuals, publications, and government heads to hasten the return of the immigrant by reminding him of his nationality and his home, and by telling him what had been happening in Greece since his departure. Periodicals carried nostalgic accounts of his village and country: "... entire eparchias [provinces] deserted and homes abandoned, lifeless roads, women without men, children

TABLE 1
IMMIGRANTS WHO DEPARTED FROM THE UNITED STATES, 1908–1931

Nationality	Number
Italians	1,240,884
Poles	339,428
English	208,081
Greeks	197,088
Germans	161,342
Magyars	156,019
Slovaks	132,763
Scandinavians[a]	125,308
Croatians and Slovenians	118,129
Russians	115,188

[a] Includes Norwegians, Danes, and Swedes.
SOURCE: *Annual Report of the Commissioner General of Immigration, Fiscal Year Ended June 30, 1931*, U.S. Department of Labor (Washington, 1931), p. 227.

without fathers, aged parents without sons, fields without laborers, churches without worshippers...." They raised fears of enforced slavery abroad, of self-banishment in an unknown land, of illness and the danger of dying in some remote spot, and of being thrown "like a dog in a grave" without the last rites of the Greek Church. Such were the dangers to which the immigrant exposed himself "in these distant shores of the New World, in this new land of the Sirens which hypnotizes the strangers with its unconquerable melody, or its gold...." There were also reminders of those who had left Greece with good intentions, but who after reaching the United States had never been heard from again. "Apart from his mother, he [the immigrant] will be lost also to his other, the great Mother, the Holy Mother, Greece."[1]

One newspaper correspondent, paying homage to the inextinguishable spirit of Hellenism, suggested that a toast be raised to the "immortal Greek spirit" which, he boasted, neither the United States, China, nor the North Pole could ever change. The same writer claimed that a special compartment would be set aside in the next world, where the departed souls of Greeks could continue their political harangues and feuds, endure their misfortunes, enjoy feasts, and perpetuate the numerous traits considered to be characteristically Greek. Coming back to earth, he insisted that in this "land of gold" that was the United States no other group was capable of maintaining its national identity as readily as the Greeks; as proof, he invited a comparison of the old-world loyalties of his compatriots with those of nationals from France, Germany, Italy, and other countries. Greeks were encouraged to preserve village customs and traditions, celebrate old-world holidays, and sing their own songs. In 1912 a Greek parliamentary committee report, in a section on the "Dangers of Assimilation," emphasized the fear that the younger the immigrant, the easier it was for him to lose his national feeling and identity. It was for the youthful immigrant that the greatest concern was shown.[2]

The more realistic among the Greeks, of whom there were many, had little faith in exhortation, the perpetuation of a particularistic spirit in the United States, or the publication of sentimental accounts of life in Greece as a means of bringing the immigrant back. Skeptics cited past events to explain what happened to those who had emigrated from their native soil. Warnings about the absorptive powers of the American nation called attention to the Italian immigrants who had gone to the United States earlier and in greater numbers. If America refused to relinquish its grip on immigrants from Italy, France, Germany, and other countries, what assurance could Greeks have that their compatriots would be released by this "land of gold"? Much had been written about the possible loss of life by drown-

---

[1] For notes to chap. 2, see pp. 141–142.

ing in the Atlantic. One shrewd observer, however, believed that Greece had far more to fear from the assimilative powers of the United States than it had from death by drowning in the ocean. From the beginning realists conceded the loss of a large segment of the emigrant population, which they believed to be among the most vigorous in the country.[3]

But events soon showed that it was neither nostalgic memories of home nor love of country that brought the first wave of immigrants back. It was the Panic of 1907 and the recession that followed. Employees on railroad construction gangs, affected by the hard times, were among the first to return. Those working in steel mills, mines, tanneries, and other industrial plants also felt the crisis. The Greek-American press carried pessimistic accounts of the discharge of Greeks and of other aliens to preserve jobs for naturalized and native-born American citizens. Many of the immigrants caught in this web of misfortune left the United States and returned home. An Athens paper estimated the total number of all nationalities departing every week for their homelands at about 25,000. Had passage been available, more would have gone, for each ship left thousands waiting behind.

Accounts of these economic difficulties appeared frequently in the Greek press, and one or two Athenian newspapers carried regular dispatches about colonies of Greeks in the United States. Letters presumably written by the immigrants themselves and printed in local papers told of the hardships endured. One such communication from St. Louis, addressed to the Greek government, recited in formal fashion how the Greeks in that community had gone there in search of wealth and had found only poverty. The letter ended as follows:

> Your obedient sons
> The five hundred Greeks of St. Louis,
> who are distressed and lack the means
> of their sustenance.

The tone of the letter, the "nonimmigrant" atmosphere it conveyed, and the quality of the writer's Greek strongly suggested that it had been written, or perhaps inspired, by some government agent.[4] Greeks in the United States also wrote about their difficulties to parents, relatives, and friends, who in turn relayed accounts to villagers and others willing to listen.

The unfortunates who managed to get home often dramatically corroborated these tales of hardship with firsthand accounts, sometimes highly colored to attract sympathy and thus compensate them for their misfortunes. A newspaper correspondent related the gloomy stories of life in the United States as told him by a group of immigrants who returned in 1908:

Yesterday morning the Austro-Americana liner Laura, arriving from New York docked in Patras where 150 Greek emigrants disembarked from the land of gold. We met many of the returned ones who gave us a melancholy picture of conditions among the Greeks there. Some who have been established in America for some time have the necessary means to support themselves, but those among the later arrivals have been faring rather poorly. Of these 150, few returned with much money. The others returned with money sent them by relatives, or by barely scraping together the necessary funds. They assured us that there are many thousands of Greeks who wish to return to their homes, but do not have the means. And not only because of this, because if they returned they would have greater difficulties since they sold what they had to go to America. Therefore they are compelled to remain there, enduring hunger with the hope that conditions might improve. They are capable of returning but fear that if they did this they would face economic disaster, especially if they learned that the economic crisis in America has ended. Others, including those who had returned, were overcome by panic and decided to return; even though they would barely eat here [in Greece] and in America gold predominates. Employment opportunities are limited. Many are working on railroad lines because they continue to be railroaders in America, but these people do not have steady work. They work three days and are laid off ten. Most of the employees have been exploited by various middlemen. The unbearable heat also affects them. If they find employment they are unable to withstand the heat. Many have died from sunstroke. In general the returned portray the conditions among the immigrants in the United States as frightful.[5]

STATUS OF REPATRIATED GREEK

Greek government officials, who had been trying from the start to check the outflow of villagers, seized upon these tales of hardship as a weapon to discourage others from leaving, and perhaps to persuade wavering ones to return. Late in 1907 the Minister of Foreign Affairs addressed a circular to all nomarchs advising them of the fate that many immigrants had encountered. Another report in 1908 told how the government had voted funds to finance the return of the destitute, described as wandering about the streets of New York and of other large cities "naked," hungry, and without places to sleep. These actions were intended to show the people that the government, despite reports to the contrary, was interested in their welfare. The hope was that potential emigrants would profit from the misfortunes of the misguided, and remain at home with their families, relatives, and friends, instead of risking their security, health, and happiness in a foreign land. The unfortunate souls brought back to Greece at government expense, the report added, owed it to humanity and to their own nation to inform their compatriots of the difficulties they had endured and the hard work they had performed in the United States, and of how they had wasted away their lives in a fruitless quest for gold and had exposed themselves to illness and death.⁶

Early in 1909 the reported plight of the immigrant in America touched off a mild international incident. Lambros Coromilas, the Greek Minister to the United States, was accused of describing America, in a report to his government, as a living "hell" where "hunger, wretchedness, despair, decay, idleness, fasting and we don't know what else" reigned supreme, and where discontented Greeks were doing everything from dying of hunger in the streets to picking rags and bones, departing for Chile, and depending on Italians for charity. Not one word, charged *Atlantis*, the Greek-American daily, did he have to say about the thousands of immigrants who were doing well and were honoring their birthplace. The report provoked George Horton, the United States Consul-General in Athens, into protesting to the Foreign Ministry against the remarks of Coromilas; he stated that on his last trip to America he had visited many immigrant communities and had found the people in a thriving condition.⁷

It was not always depression that sent immigrant Greeks back home. Love of country, the determination to help make it strong, and the willingness to fight for its defense and future greatness precipitated two volunteer return movements, a minor one in 1897 and a major one in 1912–1913. The latter episode was perhaps unparalleled in the contemporary history of the United States.

As early as 1896, the few Greeks in America were confronted with the problem of returning to their native land to fight. That year *Atlantis*, though advising Greeks to take advantage of the revival of the Olympic games to visit their homeland, acknowledged that those of military age were likely to be seized for army service. When war was declared against Turkey in 1897, Greek societies such as Tegea, Arcadia, Lycourgos, Laconia, and Sparta raised funds to finance the volunteers. *Atlantis* exhorted its readers "In the Name of God and Country" to contribute physically and financially to the support of this endeavor, and made inquiries about chartering a vessel to transport some 1,500 volunteers. Final estimates placed the number returning to Greece to fight at about 2,000, most of whom came from the United States.⁸

From 1897 to 1912 Greek peasants were relatively free to emigrate to the United States, and the evidence indicates that they took full advantage of the liberty. Beginning in 1907, however, the Greek government began contemplating measures to harness the resources of its nationals in America. That year Lambros Coromilas, whom many considered an ace diplomat, was sent to Washington to represent the Greek government. Simultaneously, plans were devised to federate the numerous Greek societies in the United States into one mighty organization, and shortly thereafter the Panhellenic Union was formed. The synchronization of these two events could hardly be dismissed as coincidental, and Greeks were enthusiastic about both developments.

Officially the aims of the Panhellenic Union were to encourage mutual aid among its members, preserve a love for the mother country, cultivate good will between the United States and Greece, stimulate the study of the English and Greek languages, foster the Greek Orthodox faith, and minister to the needs and further the best interests of Greek immigrants. This was a lofty program, couched in generalities, with which one could find little fault. But in reality, the Greek government wanted to mobilize the physical, spiritual, and financial resources of the immigrants behind the efforts of Greece. It chose the Panhellenic Union as its vehicle, and Coromilas as the man to guide the union's destinies.⁹

Before Coromilas was recalled by his government to join the cabinet of Prime Minister Eleutherios Venizelos, word arrived that Spyros Matsoukas was coming to the United States. A whirlwind money-raiser for patriotic causes, Matsoukas had stirred Greeks in Greece, Egypt, Cyprus, and elsewhere to contribute funds for the purchase of a naval craft to be donated to the Greek government. To be christened the *New Generation* to signify the reborn spirit of the day, the ship was to be in readiness to steam into Greek waters in time for the next Olympic games.

With this record of service to his country, Matsoukas was a logical choice for the task of enlisting the support of his compatriots in America. He was the foremost Greek evangelist in behalf of "faith and country." When he announced his forthcoming visit to the United States, he wrote two verses entitled "I Am Coming" and sent them to greet his countrymen in advance of his arrival. Of interest because they captured the revived Greek spirit of the day, the verses were calculated to nurture memories of the homeland. After reaching America, Matsoukas was instrumental in preserving and fostering the immigrants' ties with the mother country. He said that he was bringing the joys and tears of parents who were anxiously awaiting the return of their sons, and was carrying with him some of the sacred soil of Greece; that he hoped to soothe the sufferings of the immigrants by singing one of their native songs for them. On another occasion, he passionately exclaimed to his compatriots that what Greece needed were "guns and cannons and ships and love and strong arms. Praise and honor call for nothing else. Curses and anathemas for those who ignore their duties. Forward, boys! Our country needs money and blood to become great!"[10]

The most positive evidence of the nationalist spirit among Greeks was the volunteer units organized in numerous American cities. The first unit, formed in 1909 as a reaction against the "burning insults" the Turks were heaping on the Greeks, comprised enthusiastic young men between the ages of twenty and thirty, or often younger, who dedicated themselves to return to fight when Greece called them. These units were also intended to serve as a warning to the "cosmopolitan Greek," the man whose loyalty to his faith and country was wavering. Greece meant to live, and would live, despite such disloyalty, for her future was being propped by the arms and bayonets of her devoted sons. At first the holy zeal displayed by the members of the volunteer units proved contagious. Many Greeks flocked to the standard, apparently heedless of the mockery and ridicule heaped upon them by others who chose not to join. A national committee was formed to facilitate the work of organizing units across the country, and Greek army officers volunteered to drill the men.

The failure of Greece to declare war against Turkey in 1909, as many had expected, had a demoralizing effect on the units. Leaders found it difficult to maintain the enthusiasm of members at the high level reached when the units were first organized. During the next three years, the problem became one of keeping the organization alive. About all that could be done to boost morale was to give the units continued publicity and march them in patriotic parades. But even this was not enough. Internal bickering and endless waiting for the critical hour taxed the patience of the volunteers and all but destroyed their spirit.[11]

But events in 1912 revived their hopes for action. Late that summer war with Turkey seemed imminent. In mid-September the officers in command of the "Holy Unit of Volunteers" in New

York dispatched a cable to the Greek government inquiring about the state of Greece's foreign affairs, and suggesting that arrangements be made to receive volunteers from the United States. The American units, they claimed, consisted of about 15,000 men trained and supplied with arms. The Athens press urged all Greeks residing abroad, young and old, to return as volunteers whether they were immigrants or the offspring of immigrants.[12]

Once war was declared, excitement gripped the immigrant colonies in the United States. Many Greek-Americans were trying to make the supreme decision: "Should I return to my country to fight, or should I stay here?" *Atlantis* devoted column after column to the activities of the volunteers. Greeks who went home to fight and became veterans of the Balkan Wars have vivid stories to tell about the patriotic fervor that affected many. One such veteran described the way he and his two brothers left their places of business in Buffalo, New York, to hurry to New York City to board a vessel for Greece. But on reaching New York the three brothers found thousands of others also waiting impatiently to return. Arguments and disturbances broke out among the inflamed volunteers who vied with one another for early passage. The three brothers were compelled to remain in New York for forty days at their own expense before space became available for them. Another veteran said that he had returned to Greece by way of England because this route promised him speedier passage.

A repatriated immigrant who had spent forty-one years in the United States, but who was now a resident of one of the suburbs of Athens, described his Balkan War experiences as follows:

I left Milwaukee late in October, 1912, about October 20, to fight in the Balkan Wars. About one hundred and sixty left from Milwaukee. A doctor who was an officer in the Greek army was the leader of the unit. Many who wanted to fight were eager and green. We trained in Washington Park and in Miller's Hall. Only three Greeks from my village were killed. I think we left a good impression on the Milwaukeeans. We paraded to the depot to board a Milwaukee Road train. We were accompanied by members of the local Greek societies.

Another who had spent fourteen years in the United States and remained in Greece permanently after the war commented:

About one hundred left with me from Chicago when I left in 1913. I paid my own way. I had to wait in New York about ten days before I boarded a ship. We fought in the Epirus area. Many Greek-Americans were killed and wounded. Those who returned to fight resented the fact that the others did not come with them. Many returned to the United States after the war and took brides with them.

Still another who lived in the United States for six years and then settled in the Tripolis area, when the fighting ended, remarked:

I was president of the Los Angeles community then. I headed the one hundred and thirty-five volunteers leaving for Greece. It seemed strange to the Americans seeing the Los Angeles Greeks departing for war. About sixty were killed and wounded in Macedonia. The expenses were paid by the volunteers. Our organization didn't amount to much in Los Angeles. There were about three hundred living in Los Angeles then. At least half of those who came to fight returned to the United States.

The poor preparation of the Greek-Americans was confirmed by another volunteer:

Many who returned to fight in 1912–1913 were poorly trained. Many endured hardships. When they returned to the United States the ill effects showed up. Greece had enough men in 1912–1913. What it needed most was money.

An islander, now a resident of Mytilene, stated:

We formed a Mytilenian volunteer unit in the United States— the Lesbian Phalanx. About one hundred of the volunteers were from Plomarion which ranked next to the city of Mytilene in population. The total number in the unit was one hundred and ninety-six. We raised twelve thousand dollars to pay the costs of transportation. The money left over was divided among ourselves. News that Mytilene was liberated reached us as our ship was nearing the Azores. But we fought on Mytilene when we arrived, near Klapados.

By early 1913 the number who had returned to Greece was estimated at about 45,000. Although it was predicted that 100,000 would eventually go home to fight, later estimates placed the number actually returning at about 42,000. Figures of those wounded or killed in battle are unavailable.

When the Balkan Wars ended, and Greece was assured that her territories would be extended, the director of the Panhellenic Union warmly thanked the Greek-Americans for their sacrifices. But he also advised them that the peace was but an interlude, not the end, and that they should expect to resume the long struggle, under the leadership of King Constantine, to assimilate unredeemed territories until the national goal of a "Greater Greece" had been reached. They were asked to await the "next great call."[13]

No further military summons was forthcoming, however, and by the end of the First World War many Greek immigrants in the United States had established themselves in business and were in a position to think seriously about marriage. By this time they were in their late twenties, thirties, or early forties. Although a few of them married non-Greek women, and some took as wives young women of Greek background born of immigrant parents in the United States, most of them, especially the tradition-bound, looked toward Greece. A Greek-American wanting to marry his own kind could obtain a wife in one of two ways: through the coöperation of a relative in Greece who corresponded with him, vouched for the character of the prospective bride, arranged for an exchange of pictures, and negotiated with her parents; or by journeying to Greece himself.[14]

Why did the immigrant want a Greek wife? Why did he not marry someone in the United States? The answer was simple. Usually he believed that he would be happier with a mate of his own nationality. But there were other reasons, too. Perhaps he was unable to meet what he considered the more desirable non-Greek women—he judged the moral standards of women of other nationalities by those of some of his employees—or perhaps he was unacceptable to the non-Greek woman he would have liked to marry.

STATUS OF REPATRIATED GREEK

The immigrant also abhorred the independent airs of American women. In accordance with village custom, he believed that the husband was the head of the household, and that as the "boss" he issued instructions and expected his wife to carry them out. He had been reared on a philosophy that women occupy an obedient and subservient position in society. But in the United States he saw the reverse. A woman went out with other men before she was married, smoked cigarettes, and bobbed her hair. After marriage "she sat in the front room, put one leg on the other, and puffed on her cigarette." She fed her husband out of tin cans, put an apron on him and made him wash dishes, change the babies' diapers, scrub floors, and do other chores a self-respecting Greek male would never tolerate.

Much, if not most, of this kind of reasoning was irrational, grossly exaggerated, and based on conflicting cultural standards. But such stories circulated far and wide, and were accepted as true. It was these erroneous beliefs, plus the shortage of marriageable women of their own nationality, that caused many Greek-Americans to go back home in search of wives. The accounts told by the repatriated confirm this fact. "One reason I came back was to get married. It was difficult to marry a Greek woman in the United States in those days," conceded one. Another added: "I came here [to Greece] to marry a woman who spoke the same language I did so I could lead a happier life." A rather young but well-established Greek-American residing in Salonika volunteered this idea: "Those who married women of another nationality found it difficult to get along with them. The religious question made it difficult for me to marry one of a different nationality. Greek women are soft. They are not as bold as the American women. They respect Greek customs and traditions. Religion and nationality are deeply ingrained in them from youth." Another, residing in Tripolis, said substantially the same thing: "The American woman is free. She can leave her family and work to support herself. She takes on free airs. A Greek woman can't do this."

In addition to the desire to marry a Greek wife, existing family ties were a powerful factor in persuading many immigrants to repatriate themselves. Disillusioned and homesick wives, women in Greece unwilling to join their husbands in the United States, and anxious parents helped strengthen the immigrant's thoughts of going home and greatly accelerated the return movement.

A homesick wife was often held responsible for the husband's return to Greece, whether or not the facts substantiated the charge. A woman might be blamed for compelling an entire family to return after her husband had established himself in business in the United States. A veteran of the First World War, who went to Greece in 1919 for a visit, was married there, and returned to the United States with his bride, repatriated himself within a few years because his wife wanted to be near her parents. She was unhappy living in Chicago. A confectioner had a similar experience. He had fought in the Balkan Wars, married a village girl, and brought her to the United States where they raised a family. When the husband, a respectable citizen, successful businessman, and model parent, discovered that life in America did not appeal to his wife, he retraced his steps to Greece out of respect for her wishes and repatriated himself and his family in 1924. Standing in his Athens shop one day, he pointed to her with some pride and added: "There is the little woman for whom I left the United States."

Not all husbands, however, blamed their wives for the return to Greece. Some admitted that they were just as anxious to return. And often sickness in the family instigated the departure from the United States. One exceedingly unhappy repatriate related: "I was married to a Greek woman. She was sick. The doctor advised me to return to Greece with my wife. What could I do? We had two children. I couldn't divorce her." Frequently, too, a Greek who had left his wife and children as a young man went back to rejoin his family at an advanced age. A former Milwaukeean said, "My wife didn't want to come to the United States when the entire family could have come. Now it is too late." Another remarked, "I came back to my wife in 1923. My family wanted me back."

Repatriates frequently gave their parents as the reason for

the return to Greece. Either they were going back to see elderly parents before they died, or to make brief visits that sometimes ended in permanent residence, or to assist needy families. One immigrant went home to assume some of the responsibilities of his over-burdened and aged parents. "I was the eldest of ten children. The oldest son assumes great responsibilities in a Greek family. I helped bring two of my brothers to the United States. I had to return to help five sisters get married and to take care of my aged parents. My family looked on me as its saviour." Another commented, "I was the only son.... I came for the sake of my parents only." Still another said, "I returned to see my mother in 1927. My father died in 1923 and I didn't see him." An only son sheepishly admitted that he returned to Greece because his mother threatened to commit suicide if he didn't come home. "I didn't know any better. I believed her and came back."

Sometimes, however, the lonely and aging parent served as an excuse instead of the real reason for the repatriation of the immigrant. An individual with a cloudy reputation sentimentally stated that he returned to see his father before the latter passed away. Quoting a popular saying, he added: "When a king dies a new one takes his place; when a father dies, no one takes his place." But this same individual, who had spent more than thirty-five years in America, admitted in his less guarded moments that he had been having trouble with competitors and even with a federal agency, and that he had found it difficult to sleep at night.

The immigrant's desire to see his parents and other members of his family after an absence of years was a normal one, comparable to that which prompted many Americans to travel from state to state or from coast to coast. But if the principle was the same, the problems were more complicated for the Greek-American. The international character of his travel, the question of citizenship rights, the possibility of being unable to reënter the United States, and the necessity for cultural readjustment all posed problems of serious proportions.

Despite these difficulties, immigrants to the United States

often found it imperative to return home. Another influence tending toward repatriation, also connected with family life, was the desire of some Greek-Americans to bring up their children in Greece. Although this feeling affected only a minority of immigrants, it was strong enough and deep enough to serve occasionally as the sole reason for the return journey to the native land. These repatriates wanted their children reared in a society where they would speak the Greek language, associate with friends who had the same background, and later marry one of their own nationality. Greek-Americans sufficiently attached to the Greek way of life found fault with the seemingly independent and irresponsible children of America. In the United States it was difficult for a parent to discipline his child as sternly as he could in Greece, where Church and state worked together, and where uniformity in language, religion, custom, and tradition helped to keep the young under control. As one cleric put it: "It was a question of whether we were to remain Hellenes or become philhellenes."[15]

An apparently westernized Greek-American, who had been in the restaurant and delicatessen business for about twenty-five years, returned to Greece for two reasons. His health was poor, and he had plans for his children. "I wanted my children to preserve Greek customs and ideals. I wanted them to preserve the language and the Greek religion. I didn't want them to forget their Greek heritage. This would have been impossible to do if I remained in the United States." He returned with his wife who was a native of Greece, and his two children who were born in America.

A Peloponnesian who had been in the United States for about ten years refused to bring his family to America, blaming his lack of financial success for his inability to have his wife and children join him. Perhaps there was an element of truth in his excuse. But a son gave a different explanation, which was corroborated by his brother. The son, a small Athens merchant, said that his father was influenced by an acquaintance whose children had grown up in the United States and had disowned the Greek customs and traditions that the parents wanted to preserve. "My father was afraid the same thing would happen to us. That is why he made no effort to bring us to America. I don't call this thing unfortunate. This is a crime, but what can I do about it? My brother wanted to go to America in the worst possible way. He even wrote a letter to Mrs. Franklin D. Roosevelt offering his services to the United States Army hoping this would help him to get into the country. But it was impossible. Mrs. Roosevelt was good enough to answer. The United States Army is for American citizens. My brother is a Greek."

In recent years Greek-Americans residing in the United States, and anxious to have their children preserve Greek customs and traditions, have developed a different technique. They take their sons and daughters to live in Greece for a year or two. One prospective repatriate left for Greece with his wife and two children, who were born in the United States. One of the children was a boy in his early teens, the other a girl of four. The boy attended a Greek school but was extremely unhappy. In fact, the father and mother were themselves dissatisfied with life in Greece and all four returned to the United States. But they felt compensated for the expense and trouble of their journey, for the children had seen the birthplace of their parents, and had strengthened their knowledge of the Greek language.

Sometimes the immigrant himself preferred the Greek way of life to the American. It is likely that many repatriates were moved by such sentiments, though relatively few were prepared to admit it. The few who did concede a preference for Greece, however, probably answered for those who remained silent. "I realized that life in the United States wasn't what I wanted," remarked a Cretan. "I was thirty-one years old when I went to the United States. When I returned I was forty-one. I felt I wanted to settle in Greece permanently." A Macedonian admitted: "I liked life in Greece...it was easier...." Another who contended that he had always planned to make his permanent home in Greece explained: "My mind was here all the time. My brothers were successful in business. I had a girl friend I knew for years. I also had a girl friend in the United States who was married to someone else. I wasn't happy in the United States."

Climate and health were factors that occasionally entered into an immigrant's decision to return to his native land. Like other migrating peoples, the Greeks who came to the United States ignored isothermic lines. Had they followed these temperature indicators they would have settled in the southern states. But instead of seeking a climate comparable to that of the Peloponnesus, the Greek islands, and Sterea Hellas, they established themselves in the East, the North, and the Middle West, where they were exposed to rigorous winter cold and intense summer heat. It was small wonder that they longed for the more hospitable climate of Greece.

The hope of recovering one's health was also mentioned as a reason for repatriation. Said one returned Greek-American in a positive and defensive tone: "I had stomach trouble. Ill health was the reason. There was no other reason." Another reported: "My doctor advised me to change my climate. I returned to my village and drank camomile. Camomile helped make me well. So did the change in diet...." In a similar tone, a repatriate remarked: "I couldn't stand the climate. I was in the restaurant business. The kitchen odors hurt me. My doctor advised me to leave for Greece." A Rhodian said, "I fell from a ladder while I was painting. I came to Greece because I could receive treatment from a good specialist." An elderly widow said that her husband, a sponge diver in Tarpon Springs, collapsed and died within six or seven months after his return. "So many who return from America are tired and broken in health."

A veteran of the First World War struck a note that was absent from the comments of most of the returned immigrants. He complained of the poor treatment he had received in a veterans' hospital. He charged discrimination against him, and accused the hospital of subjecting him to experimental treatments; for this he blamed Jewish doctors and Jewish influences in American life. Believing that his health would improve, he left the hospital against medical advice, and returned to Greece.

Perhaps responsible for some of the health problems were the long hours of work in America, which made many immigrants feel the need for leading a more relaxed life. "I worked too hard," remarked a trucker in Tripolis. "I was a fruit peddler and climbed many stairs. The United States was good to me. But I got tired of rising early in the morning to go to the green market and climbing the stairs I climbed in Chicago." The wife of a repatriated immigrant explained how she and her husband opened their restaurant early in the morning and worked until midnight every day, Saturdays, Sundays, and holidays. "He [the husband] couldn't stand it any longer."

Possibly to enjoy a respite from tedious working conditions, or to regain their health in a salubrious climate, or to see aging parents, many Greek-Americans went home for a brief visit, intending to return after a short time to the United States. A surprisingly large number of these visitors, however, became permanent residents of Greece.

This kind of repatriated immigrant often explained his actions in his own uninhibited way. "I came to see my relatives and then return to the United States. I became sick and I also got married," remarked one. An embittered Dodecanesean who fell sick in Rhodes shortly after his arrival said, "I had a case pending in court. I had no faith in my lawyer." Another disillusioned repatriate commented: "I just came for a short visit in 1932. I expected to return to the United States in a short time. But a friend of mine persuaded me to stay. In 1935 I was married. I should never have returned to Greece." Still another said: "I came to see Greece. I was married and we have been 'eating bread' ever since." A rather contented Peloponnesian explained: "My father died and I had an orphan sister. I had some property I was interested in. I planned to stay six months because I had a six-months leave of absence from my job. I helped my sister get married and I was married too. Life appealed to me in Greece." A First World War veteran nonchalantly remarked, "I also came to see my parents and decided to cast my anchor."

The Great Depression of 1929–1933 had less effect on the volume of traffic from the United States to Greece than might have been expected. Some immigrants departed with their

American savings because business opportunities were slack and this was as good a time as any to go to Greece, but not because they were destitute, hungry, and homeless. There were, of course, some exceptions. A tattered-looking individual, who had lived in Gary, Indiana, from 1928 to 1931 admitted that he returned to Greece because he was unemployed and without friends. An ex-villager from the Patras area told a dramatic tale of frustration and reverses. Like many others he had been in the restaurant business. He started restaurants on three different occasions, and failed each time. Disgusted with life and "broke," he managed to obtain some money from his father-in-law to return to Greece temporarily to see what conditions were like. After a brief stay, he wanted to go back to the United States and rejoin his wife. But he discovered that this was impossible. Besides lacking the cash, he had failed to become an American citizen. Within time he also learned that his wife had divorced him, which came as a great shock.

There were many repatriates whose reasons for returning to Greece cannot be easily classified, because they extended over so wide a range. A substantial number returned during the 1920's because living costs were high in the United States and low in Greece. These repatriates reported that an individual could live in reasonable comfort, Greek style, on $60 or $70 a month. Other explanations for going back to live in the old country varied from the craving for recognition in one's home village to restlessness and inability to remain very long in one place.

A resident of Volos who came into contact with numerous Greek-Americans explained that "Many of these people expected to receive recognition when they returned to Greece. This was a factor in the actions of many who were just part of a large mass in the United States." A recently returned Greek-American operating several launderettes in Athens admitted that he preferred Greece because, as he said, "Here I am king, in the United States I wasn't anybody."

At least two repatriated Greek-Americans found it difficult to justify their decision to return. A Cretan said, "I met a friend who was going to Greece and on the spur of the moment I decided I would go too. I planned to stay five or six months. But when I got to Greece I was married within that time." When a man who had spent seventeen years in the United States was asked why he returned, he replied: "It is hard to explain why. I just can't answer. I ask myself this every day. It must have been the craze of the day. Many Greeks were leaving for Greece and I thought I would do the same." An American Legion officer explained it this way: "It is just a plain lack of common sense that so many of us have suffered from. Instead of remaining where we were faring reasonably well, we decided to risk all we had for the sake of seeing old friends and old places."

The number of Greek-Americans willing to risk their future against the doubts and uncertainties of repatriation—whether for reasons of health or climate or livelihood or family or marriage—was quite substantial. Unfortunately, accurate statistical data are unavailable. As noted above, defining a Greek posed a problem because those who emigrated from Turkey were classified as Greek by Greek authorities and as Turks by the Americans. Immigration figures were misleading also because the many immigrants who made more than one round-trip voyage were included in more than one compilation. Official Greek sources likewise claimed that only those who traveled as third-class passengers were tabulated as immigrants by the American authorities. Usually those who returned to Greece were in better economic condition than they had been when they first left for the United States; hence the large but not necessarily preponderant number who went back as second-class passengers were not counted as returning immigrants. Also unaccounted for were those who made their exit illegally.[16]

Beginning July 1, 1907, the United States kept a record of all immigrant aliens departing for foreign lands. Although official records for earlier years are unavailable, it is believed that for some time the immigrant outflow had been about one-third of the inflow. According to the Trans-Atlantic Passenger Association, from 1899 to 1910 about thirty-seven steerage passengers left the United States for Europe for every hundred such passengers brought into the United States from Europe.

During the early years, the number of Greek immigrant aliens leaving the United States fell considerably below the general average for all nationalities. Of the 88,205 Greeks admitted from 1908 to 1910, some 21,852, or about 25 per cent, departed. Of all the eastern Mediterranean and Asiatic peoples, the Greeks were the least inclined to leave. By contrast, more than half the Koreans, Chinese, Turks, Magyars, Croatians, and South Italians entering during these years left the United States, and a relatively smaller number of the Irish, Jews, Welsh, Scotch, Armenians, Bohemians, Moravians, Dutch, Flemish, English, Ruthenians, Portuguese, Lithuanians, and Scandinavians.[17]

The number of Greek immigrants who reached the United States between 1908 and 1923 has been placed officially at 366,454. Of this total, 168,847 made a return trip to Greece with the intention of repatriating themselves. In other words, over the sixteen-year period about 46 per cent declared their intention of returning to live in Greece, whereas 197,607, or 54 per cent, indicated that they planned to remain in the United States. Except for the periods 1911–1914 and 1919–1921 when, as noted above, departures were abnormally heavy, emigration from the United States to Greece totaled less than 10,000 during most years. After 1924 the return movement to Greece was negligible, reaching its lowest level during the depression and the New Deal years.[18]

A comparison of the emigration of Greek aliens in terms of "race and people" with the emigration in terms of "country of future intended residence" reveals some marked disparities, especially for the years 1908–1913 (see table 2). Greek aliens left the United States with apparently no intention of living in Greece. Several hundred such emigrants departed annually from 1908 to 1910 inclusive, more than 1,700 annually from 1911 to 1912, and 953 during 1913. These people either planned to reside in some country other than Greece, or else considered themselves Greeks but were returning to homes in Ottoman-occupied territory. More likely the latter was true, because after 1913, when at the end of the Balkan Wars Greece received a substantial amount of former Turkish territory in Europe, the disparity dropped considerably.

A breakdown in the available statistics for 1920, a fairly representative year, discloses the age brackets, the disproportionate number of males, and the length of time the prospective repatriates spent in the United States. Of the 20,319 departing in 1920, the year of the second largest outflow, 19,051 were males and 1,268 were females. Some 15,128 ranged from sixteen to forty-four years in age, and 4,918 were forty-five years of age or older. More than half, or 11,779, had lived in the United States from five to ten years; 6,222 for five years or less; 1,729 from ten to fifteen years; 488 from fifteen to twenty years; and 101 for more than twenty years. In general, of those who returned to Greece during the fiscal year ending in 1920, almost 70 per cent had resided in the United States for five or more years. Many, if not most, of them had come to the United States in their teens and were returning to Greece as mature men. Almost nineteen out of every twenty were males who had seen more of life in the United States than their wives, because they worked in factories and stores while the women stayed close to their circle of Greek acquaintances.

Few naturalized citizens of the United States departed for permanent residence in Greece; there were, for example, only 158 such citizens out of the total of 20,319 Greeks who departed during the fiscal year 1920. Of these, the majority were males between the ages of sixteen and forty-four who had lived in the United States for five or more years. Eighty-five of the 158 had lived in the country ten or more years. In short, once a Greek had become a citizen of the United States he was less inclined to leave.[19]

The amount of money the repatriated immigrant took back to Greece varied in accordance with the date of his arrival in the United States, the length of his residence, his personal spending habits, and the type of work he performed. Usually,

TABLE 2
COMPARISON, BY FISCAL YEAR, OF GREEK EMIGRANT ALIENS DEPARTED WITH EMIGRANT ALIENS DEPARTED WHO GAVE GREECE AS COUNTRY OF INTENDED FUTURE RESIDENCE, 1908-1952

Year	Greek emigrant aliens departed	Emigrant aliens departed who gave Greece as country of intended future residence
1908	6,763	6,131
1909	6,275	5,606
1910	8,814	8,144
1911	11,134	9,376
1912	13,323	11,461
1913	31,556	30,603
1914	11,266	11,124
1915	9,767	9,775
1916	4,855	4,829
1917	2,082	2,034
1918	2,952	2,986
1919	15,562	15,482
1920	20,319	20,314
1921	13,470	13,423
1922	7,649	7,506
1923	3,060	2,988
1924	7,335	7,250
1925	6,659	6,574
1926	5,188	5,164
1927	3,140	3,130
1928	2,525	2,461
1929	1,793	1,736
1930	785	733
1931	816	753
1932	1,607	1,406
1933	1,402	1,277
1934	721	644
1935	450	402
1936	842	807
1937	406	374
1938	477	460
1939	493	470
1940	280	261
1941	85	77
1942	17	6
1943	2	1
1944	18	0
1945	17	3
1946	94[a]	111[a]
1947	410[a]	470[a]
1948	354	349
1949	444	389
1950	511[a]	588[a]
1951	358[a]	374[a]
1952	...[b]	435

[a] The apparent inconsistency in these data exists in the source.
[b] Data are not available.
SOURCES: *Annual Reports of the Commissioner General of Immigration*, 1908-1932; *Statistical Abstract of the United States*, 1932-1952.

the longer his stay the larger the amount of money he saved. For instance, two brothers residing in the United States from 1906 to 1909 accumulated $1,500; another immigrant, a resident of Chicago from 1906 to 1912, returned with about $6,000; one who had been an American resident for seventeen years took back $12,000 in 1926; and another who had come to America as a youth of fourteen in 1914 returned in 1922 with $3,000. Still others were able to save as much as $20,000, $30,000, and $40,000. It was estimated that two successful businessmen took anywhere from $2,000 to $100,000 to Greece. These figures do not include the remittances immigrants sent to relatives while they were still residing in the United States.

Even though the aggregate sum brought back will never be known, the assumption is that the overwhelming majority of immigrants returned with some money. The lot of the economically unsuccessful repatriate might be a very unhappy one, from a social as well as a financial standpoint. A minority came back empty-handed, returning because they were able to borrow money; others who would have liked to return hesitated to do so from fear of being ridiculed by friends and relatives because they had little to show for their years of hard labor in America.[20]

As a rule, the repatriate was a small businessman, a restaurant operator and a confectioner, or an employee in some industrial plant or shop. There were few professional men of stature in the return movement, except for a number of dentists and engineers. Because the immigrant contributed little to the scholarly and artistic world, there were no musicians, scientists, literary figures, or scholars. Substantially wealthy businessmen were conspicuous by their absence. It is difficult to imagine such persons wanting to return to Greece when fortune had smiled upon them, except when they had to sell out their interests, as had one or two of the Greek-American tobacco men during earlier years. The better rooted a person was socially and economically, the less inclined he was to leave the United States. By a simple process of elimination it was the small businessman, the shopkeeper, the construction-gang worker, and others with few or no binding family ties in the United States who left. A day laborer with a large family and few funds had little choice except to remain. The cost of transporting his family to Greece was prohibitive, even if his wish to return was great. Perhaps here was one occasion when immobility proved a blessing.²¹

When the repatriates returned to Greece, their economic condition was better than it had been when they left for America. This was apparent in the style in which they traveled, in their attire, and in the air of confidence they displayed. If traveling in third class was good enough for them when they first left for the United States, it was beneath a good many of them on the return voyage. Some came back by way of England, Germany, France, and Italy. Displaying a spirit of optimism, they built up their exuberance to a point where they could be disappointed at the slightest turn of their fortunes.

It is fairly easy to understand why more Greek-Americans did not return to their native land. There was among them a growing awareness that it would be difficult to reënter the United States once they had left; the Greek language press carried frequent dispatches of the proposed immigration bars, and only the most indifferent could afford to take these lightly. The defeat suffered by Greece in Asia Minor in 1922 had a crippling effect on the morale of many expatriated Greeks who began disassociating themselves from the mother country. Unfavorable accounts of the experiences of those who had gone to Greece with the intention of remaining also trickled back into American communities of Greeks. Most important was the fact that the majority of the immigrants found the United States the land of their choice and decided to become a permanent part of it. Whatever their difficulties when they first arrived, America was preferred as a country in which to live and raise a family. The great stress placed on naturalization after the First World War was a reflection of this attitude.

The fact that so many chose to remain in America did not please Greek nationalists, who saw that these expatriates would be lost to Greece. It was once believed that the Greek was uninfluenced by foreign surroundings and that, like Odysseus after an absence of years, he too would return from his wanderings happy to see smoke rising from his father's home. This almost childlike faith in the return of the immigrant was based chiefly on the experiences of those who had gone to Turkey, Egypt, Rumania, Bulgaria, and other neighboring countries where they maintained a fiery national spirit. The nationalists failed to take into account that in some of these older areas, which were also nearer home, the standard of living was lower than in certain parts of Greece, and that other forces helped make the Greek want to preserve his national identity. On the other hand, experiences in the United States indicated that after the lapse of a few years the immigrant found it difficult to avoid some degree of assimilation, especially when he enjoyed a standard of living that was much higher than the one he had known in his native land.[22]

The actual departure for Greece was a much anticipated event. Often it was preceded by a series of receptions or feasts, when friends from the same or nearby villages would gather to bid the returning immigrant farewell, to load him with gifts to take to their respective relatives, and most likely to give him envelopes containing money for brothers, sisters, aunts, or uncles at home. Village songs might be sung, happenings of yesteryears told and retold. Before long the repatriate would be on board the ship that would carry him home. In a fortnight or so he would be back with his parents, relatives, and friends, feasting with them after an absence of years, visiting old haunts, swapping stories in the village square or coffeehouse, and perhaps "strutting his stuff" as one of the village boys who had made good. Life would be relaxed. Punching a time clock, heeding the warnings of a foreman, or working abnormally long hours in his store would be a thing of the past. There would be the afternoon siesta, the various religious holidays to be observed again, and the opportunity to be in the hospitable atmosphere of his native land among his own kind of people. If he was single, matrimonially anxious friends and relatives would busy themselves helping him find a desirable mate. These were the reflections that filled the minds and hearts of Greek-Americans as they were about to embark for the return voyage to Greece.

CHAPTER THREE

READJUSTMENT IN GREEK SOCIETY

Since the repatriate often returned in a highly emotional frame of mind, he gave little thought to the problems of living in Greece after having lived in the most highly industrialized nation in the world, where the code of ethics, social relationships, and the outlook on life were different. The first impressions, often indelible ones, were bound to be influenced by his experiences in passing through customs, the amount of the first cab fare he paid, his stay in a hotel, the general appearance of Greece, the persistence of ubiquitous relatives, and perhaps the staring of curious Greeks. This set of circumstances could easily have been the beginning of a sequence of unhappy experiences for one who was returning home.

The sentimental repatriate often took his first view of the Greek mainland or of an island with tears in his eyes. For years he had praised this heroic land, the people, the climate, and the Greek way of life. Now after a long absence he was coming home, and his hopes ran high. Besides expecting a hearty welcome, he hoped to find tangible evidence of progress. Certainly, he thought, there must have been changes in the way business was conducted, in sanitation, transportation, and the handling of foods; and perhaps there would even have been a quieting down in the rancorous debates of the Greek politicians who involved the nation in one political squabble after another.

Although the Greek-American had come a long way and had

lived abroad for a number of years, he was still provincial in contrast to the seasoned European or American traveler who was accustomed to the small practices to which foreigners were subjected. For all practical purposes the repatriate was as much a stranger as the latter, but he was of a different type and in an excitable frame of mind. He could easily rebel against practices which others would dismiss with a shrug of the shoulders or a laugh. He considered himself a loyal son who was dutifully returning home, and as such he wanted to be treated with respect. He had a knowledge of the language and, unlike the admiring tourist, he was in a position to understand the peculiar as well as to admire the good. And often he lacked humility.[1]

The returning repatriate was usually stocked with large quantities of clothing, shoes, and personal wares which he had accumulated over a period of years. One hopeful individual, whose ambitions never materialized, amassed clothing and personal effects with the same spirit that a matrimonially ambitious young girl built her trousseau. Often the immigrant returned with gifts for relatives he had not seen since his departure for the United States.

Those who passed through customs during the 1920's complained of pettiness, rudeness, officiousness, and dishonesty on the part of the attending clerks. One repatriate described the customs office as a farce. "There was much pilfering, arbitrariness, etc. I paid fifty thousand drachmas in duties in 1926 when I returned." Another who came at an earlier time described it as a travesty. "There was ... confusion. I came to Greece in 1912 to fight in the Balkan Wars and at my expense. Despite this, I was detained ... for about a day."

To what extent the complaints of the repatriates were justified will perhaps never be known. No doubt some of them exaggerated their experiences, and others may have deserved the treatment they received. In all probability the volatile temper of officials, the confusion that characterized the customs office, and the endless waiting and wrangling taxed the patience of

---

[1] For notes to chap. 3, see pp. 142–143.

many who reëntered Greece. A gendarmery officer, who went to the United States in an official capacity and then returned to Greece, remarked:

The customs office has given the returned Greek-American a hard time. I think the number trying to bring goods into the country illegally are few. What a few have done has made many others suffer.

After an absence of years these people return armed with gifts for their relatives and clothes and other articles for their personal use. They bring these clothes, shoes, underwear, shirts, and other personal apparel because of a feeling of insecurity. They stock up for future years. Greece has had a series of wars and the people want to be prepared. They know they would have a hard time obtaining these articles in Greece. They also know that if their money is gone there are few places for them to work. That is why they make such preparations.

Other Greeks, of course, adopted a less charitable attitude toward the repatriate. Sometimes the hypercritical placed him in the same category as the Greek-American tourist and the black-market operator of the post-World War II period. Often the illicit activities of others were blamed on the repatriate.

The immigrant who returned to Greece after the First World War was required to serve in the army. Greece's military and political leaders were prepared to tackle the "last leg" in the march toward fulfillment of the imperial goal. The next to the "last leg" had been completed in 1913 when the Greeks emerged victorious from the Balkan Wars. From 1920 to 1922 they needed all the military and financial support they could muster to make the ill-fated attempt to incorporate Constantinople, the historic capital of the Byzantine Empire, and other unredeemed territory into a Greater Greece.[2] This project ended in disaster in 1922.

Even those who had served with the United States Army during the war and had become American citizens were subject to military duty. A war veteran who returned in 1924 said: "I had to pay the equivalent of a hundred dollars for not serving in the Greek army; however, a law was passed enabling those who served with allied forces to count this as past service. I lacked six months." Another commented: "When I returned to Greece I believed that all who served in the allied forces would be exempt from serving in the Greek army. After two years I was compelled to serve for six months and paid something to discharge the remaining eight months required by law."

Greek-Americans who were United States citizens, or thought they were, protested against military service and took their grievances to the office of the American Consul in Athens. Usually, they were told to comply with the requests of local Greek authorities, although the Consul tried to protect the rights of American citizens as best he could under the circumstances. When aid was extended, the Greek-American was required to protest his conscription and swear to the proper United States authorities that he was serving against his will, and that he had not taken an oath of allegiance to the Greek king or done anything else that was inconsistent with American citizenship. The Consul might not be able to relieve the American citizen of serving in the Greek army, but he could assure him of some protection of his citizenship rights. Obviously, such consular aid was extended only to the small minority who had acquired citizenship status before returning and had not been absent from the United States beyond the legally prescribed time.[3]

Large numbers of returning Greek-Americans settled in the Peloponnesus, especially in the provinces of Arcadia, Laconia, and Messenia, from which the exodus was heaviest during the years of emigration. The villages near Tripolis were filled with Greek-Americans. Many repatriates lived in and around Patras. Except for the greater Athens area, to which untold numbers flocked, fewer repatriates returned to the cities and villages of Sterea Hellas. A fair representation of Greek-Americans established themselves in Salonika, but in general few returned to Macedonia, Epirus, and Thrace, disputed territories from which many had fled before the Balkan Wars. Substantial numbers also returned to Crete, Karpathos, and Rhodes in the Dodecanese, and to Mytilene, Chios, and other islands scattered throughout the eastern Mediterranean and Aegean seas. The island of Karpathos, particularly in view of its size and population, had an impressive number of Greek-Americans.

Perhaps the majority settled in the metropolitan areas of Athens, Salonika, Piraeus, and Patras, and in and around the smaller cities of Tripolis, Kalamas, and Pyrgos. No doubt the choice of residence was influenced by the urban life the immigrant had led in the United States, and by the influx of population from rural areas to the city, which was affecting Greece as it was other countries of the world.

But the villages were by no means ignored. One writer remarked that at one time the principal daily task in his village was that of preparing to send someone to or receive someone from the United States. Employees of the United States government who were in Greece on assignments, as well as travelers and visitors, claimed there were few villages without at least one former American resident. As a rule, a repatriated Greek-American who heard that an American was in the neighborhood made a point of locating the visitor, identifying himself, and recapitulating his experiences in New York, Detroit, Chicago, or any other city in which he might have lived. Available data on social security, railroad retirement, and veteran benefit payments indicate that returned immigrants were scattered widely in the villages of the mainland and island areas of Greece.

Although our discussions have centered on the immigrant returning from the United States, it should be remembered that repatriates from America constituted but a small fraction of the total. Thousands came from other countries, some voluntarily and others involuntarily, during and after the First World War. The outbreak of the Russian Revolution in 1917 marked the start of a population influx from Odessa, the Crimea, and other regions near the Black Sea. Nationalist tensions in southern and eastern Europe, as well as in the Middle East, aroused fears among Greeks living there and encouraged many of them to depart for Greece. Some of the generalizations about Greek-American repatriates will have applicability to these immigrants returning from other lands, but our primary intent here is to investigate the motivations and problems and adjustments of Greeks coming home from the United States to live.

Greek-Americans who expected to receive a hero's welcome in Greece from persons other than members of their immediate families were bound to be disappointed. After the First World War, momentous issues growing out of the conflict, the Greek imperial dream, and the bitter quarrel between King Constantine and Eleutherios Venizelos faced the country. The rout of the Greeks in Asia Minor by the Turks, and the need for absorbing one and a half million refugees dwarfed everything else, including returned immigrants, into insignificance. The press was in the best position to concern itself with Greek-Americans and their problems, but it was involved in party strife and disturbed about the tangled state of the nation's foreign and domestic affairs.[4]

Even when recognition was forthcoming, it was not exactly what the repatriate had expected. The reaction toward returning Greek-Americans in the Athens area, and to a lesser extent in the smaller cities, was one of scorn commingled with envy. Often the better-educated Greek dismissed the repatriate as a nondescript person, disparaging him in private as a former sheepherder or goatherd who had turned immigrant, become a lunchroom man, a bootblack, or a confectionery store operator in the United States, worked hard, saved money, and returned to Greece. Except for the money he brought back, he had advanced socially and intellectually little beyond his status at the time of his departure. He was a person of little education. His Greek was as poor as ever, and his English even worse. A favorite saying was, "He left as a young donkey and returned as an older one," advanced in years but not in wisdom.

In the rural areas, the repatriate was likely to receive a genuine "welcome home" from members of his family and from others who expected favors. Short-lived monthly publications such as *Malebos* and *Oinountios*, yearbooks published by a former villager who had become a professional man, nationalist organs anxious to retain the support of all immigrants, and a few provincial newspapers published in communities that had benefited from remittances, all devoted space to the repatriate. But this recognition was too limited in amount and too specialized in character to bring great satisfaction.[5]

The Greeks coined meaningful phrases to describe the Greek-American. Most common was "Brooklis," a corruption of Brooklynite. Because many of the immigrants who returned in the early days had come from Brooklyn, the Greeks assumed that all those who went to the United States lived there; hence any Greek-American was a "Brooklis." "Kounesmenos," or "shaken one," was another popular name. The immigrant was presumed to have been shaken by his ocean travel, or perhaps so jarred by his American experiences that he no longer fitted into the Greek scene. Some even suggested that the eccentric behavior of the Greek-American probably stemmed from the hard labor he had performed in the United States. Less popular, but occasionally used, were expressions such as "vlamenos," or "afflicted one"; "yankee-des"; "how-ja-lakides," a corruption of "how do you like this"; "all-right boys"; "okay-boys"; "hello-boys"; "yes-yes-yes"; "Johnides"; and just plain "Americanoi."

Some Americans in Athens were amused bystanders during this reception of Greek-Americans by Greeks, but other Americans occasionally joined in the name-calling fest. They, too, characterized the returned immigrants as "obnoxious," "arrogant," "mean people," "show-offs," "less tolerant than intelligent Americans," "boorish," "number one problem children," and as "persons who belonged in a class by themselves." Often the Americans acquired these sentiments from Athenian acquaintances who were notorious in their contempt for the immigrant classes, and were perhaps influenced by their inability to find a justifiable explanation as to why anyone would want to leave the United States and come to Greece to live.[6]

The Greek-American was frequently ridiculed after his return to his native land, because of ways of speech and dress and behavior he had picked up in the United States. He was easy to recognize, at least during the early months of his return. Often his dress was gaudy, compared with the somber attire of the Greek. He shaved oftener, had his hair cut differently, walked faster, and employed a terminology that was part of the Greek-American dialect. The repatriate's ridiculous attempt to pose as an authority on English, his flaunting of two or three fountain pens and of three or four rings, his gold watch chain, gold teeth, silk shirt, stiff collar, "loud-colored" tie, and American-style shoes made him a ready target. A dentist reported the story of "a Greek-American who filled his mouth with gold crowns to show that he had money...."[7]

Authoritarian airs assumed by those who had lived in the United States were obnoxious. "Those who returned ... never knew what American life was," remarked one shrewd observer. "They came back and posed as though they did. The local people knew this and laughed at them." Although the immigrant might not have farmed since he had left Greece, he believed that his stay in the United States qualified him to speak on agriculture with authority. Not all the returned immigrants behaved in this way, and no doubt the stories told about those who did were often exaggerated. Those who flaunted their knowledge of America, however, brought down upon themselves, and upon the innocent as well, the wrath of the local people.

In view of the friction that occasionally marred the relations between repatriates and Greeks who had never left their native land, it is pertinent to consider the reactions of returned immigrants to the people and life of Greece. Such reactions varied over a wide range, from complete satisfaction through mere acceptance all the way to extreme unhappiness. The variation depended on numerous factors, the date of the immigrant's return, the experiences he had had, the place where he had lived in the United States, and the temper of the times.

A surprisingly large number of immigrants said that they found life in Greece agreeable. One who repatriated himself immediately after the Balkan Wars remarked: "Money was worth much more then. People weren't as desperate then as they are now [1953]." Another said that in 1912 "Life in Greece was pretty good. I liked it." Still another, who went to his native village to live after the First World War, said, "It wasn't too bad. I didn't lack much. I had been back and forth several times. Life was reasonably pleasant. I had the means to provide myself with the comforts villagers have."

Some repatriates frankly admitted that they were unhappy in Greece during the first few months or years. A Peloponnesian who had lived in the United States from 1899 to 1913, and then had returned to the same general part of Greece, commented: "Life was empty. It didn't appeal to me. It was almost zero existence...." Said another who returned in 1927: "Life appeared peculiar. This wasn't what I had grown accustomed to in the United States. It took me three or four years to adjust myself. People are difficult to deal with in Greece. It is not like the United States. There is the Greek psychology, the poverty, the sight of the poor, and the sharp practices you have to deal with." Another repatriate, returning at approximately the same time, stated:

I decided to come to Athens to live. Life in Tripolis and in the village was unappealing. I preferred the city life I knew in the United States.

The people seemed untidy. The stores were poorly kept. The food was unappetizing. Sanitation was lacking. You had little confidence in the people. Greece then had many refugees from Asia Minor and that complicated matters.

It took me about one and a half to two years to adjust myself to Greece. Everything was at fault.... My wife and I took trips to regain our senses. We should have returned to the United States then. But we bought a new home that was completely modern. This made me more content.

Others corroborated these reports of unhappiness suffered by immigrants after their return to Greece. One who spent twenty-two years in the United States and returned to Crete in 1936 said: "I came to my village to live. Life seemed hard. I didn't like it." A former laborer and steelworker remarked: "I didn't like it here.... There was the poverty, the taxes, and the people who were different from those I knew in America." Still another who had spent forty-one years in the United States and had settled in a suburb of Athens claimed: "Life seemed peculiar to me. I found it different from what it had been presented to me as being. Those who had been to Greece and then went back to America spread misleading optimistic reports about conditions. They probably wanted others to endure what they did. The village I knew wasn't there; it was different."

A Greek-American who returned to live in Navpaktos in 1927 commented: "I took special baths, I inhaled vapors, I traveled to the mountains. Life is what you make it. Life is good in Greece but you have to keep yourself buttoned. The local Greek says this fellow knows his way back to the United States to get more money if what he has runs out."

Some of the repatriates felt that the cheaper cost of living in Greece compensated them in large part for the difficulties they encountered. One critical individual, after finding fault with various phases of life, admitted that in 1927 "With fifty dollars a month a person could live very comfortably. This was considered a good income then." A Macedonian residing in the Salonika area confirmed this statement, and added: "It was even better in 1937. It was possible for a person to live well with his family on seventy-five to a hundred dollars a month. A single person could live on half of this."

The customary procedure for the repatriate was to visit his family, usually in a village, and perhaps remain there until he decided where he was going to establish himself permanently. The length of his stay in the village depended chiefly on his parents, relatives and friends, property interests, and his personal reactions. Next to the army, which might have first claim on the repatriate, it was family influence that weighed most heavily on any decision he made. If rural life satisfied him, or if he was unable to decide where he wanted to go, he usually followed the path of least resistance and remained with his parents or relatives.

The return of a son or a nephew furnished the setting for a family reunion; brothers, sisters, cousins, uncles, and aunts from nearby villages and towns gathered to see him after an absence of years. "They were pleased. My brothers in particular were pleased," said one. "I was welcomed.... Living with relatives was possible and permissible," admitted another. "I was welcomed and embraced," jokingly remarked one Greek-American. "My relatives killed chickens and lambs for me. I was also watched like a hawk to see in which direction I would go."

Naturally some fared better than others with their relatives, either because their kin were well-to-do, or because they were so happy to see the wanderer home again that little else mattered. A few of the returning immigrants were warned in advance to be on guard. A former lunchroom operator residing in Larissa explained: "I was forewarned prior to my leaving the United States by an uncle. I was advised to pity no one, and not to advance money to relatives when I got to Greece." Later arrivals profited from the experiences of earlier ones. "In those early days few people warned you about being on guard against your relatives. Now the Greek-Americans are more careful."

But most returned immigrants faced families who had a reputation for being demanding as well as hospitable. This usually occurred in villages where poverty abounded, and hence where a flock of relatives were on hand to greet the repatriate. "I was regarded as a wealthy American who returned with his pockets filled," explained a Rhodian. "My relatives were poor. All expected help from me. But I was unable to do much for them," remarked one. "They expected help. I helped them. I was asked for help continuously," stated another. "I was well received because I had money," complained a former confectioner. "You have to be careful. Relatives and friends come around and suggest that you do this or that. I escaped this," observed a coffeehouse manager. A less fortunate repatriate remarked: "My friends and relatives said I was of no use to them because I didn't bring them any help."

A repatriate often discovered that the hospitality of a relative or a villager represented a form of investment from which the host expected a return, either for himself, or for someone else whose cause he was advancing. Little time was lost before the long-lost brother from America was presented with a polite request for a so-called loan, which God and the borrower would repay him many times over. Occasionally the solicitor was a professed relative whom the returned immigrant had neither seen nor heard of until he came to the village. This loan or gift, as it frequently turned out to be, was intended for one or more of several purposes: to pay a mortgage; to purchase a donkey or a horse; to educate a brother, a son, or a nephew; to provide a dowry for a sister or a niece.

Borrowers employed various techniques in eliciting these loans. Usually the would-be benefactor was invited to a dinner which was attended by a host of relatives and friends, or perhaps by a prospective bride and her parents, or merely by a representative of the latter. Sometimes the request was put directly to the repatriate by the village priest (who frequently served as the middleman), a cousin, an uncle, an aunt, the person who had sponsored him when he was baptized, or a close personal friend. One repatriate described how he was "wined and dined," and how his host "sprang his secret" before he had a chance to leave.

Once the plea for aid had been made, there followed endless visitations enlivened by melodramatic accounts of hardship and poverty, which were accompanied by groans of agony and reassurances of payment. This type of solicitation was common, and became part of the ritual of repatriation to which many returned immigrants were subjected. The cost of the initiation usually was a sum equivalent to that advanced to the defaulting borrower. A loan was difficult, if not impossible, to collect.

Observers, as well as the returned immigrants, gave accounts of the ordeals to which Greek-Americans were subjected. One of the most fantastic involved an individual whose relatives pressed him so hard for aid that he sought refuge in the Mt. Athos area, the historic site of the monks. Another concerned a wealthy visitor whose relatives and friends watched his movements closely and even gathered in his hotel lobby to waylay him with invitations and proposals of various sorts. An American-born woman of non-Greek lineage, married to a Greek and residing in Athens, observed that these requests for aid sent many Greek-Americans scurrying to the cities to escape from such solicitations. Another observer described the relatives as "a big pain in the neck." Although conceding that "Some Greek-Americans exaggerate their experiences," he went on to say, "But I know of cases where things were not exaggerated. They [the relatives] rob you, lie to you, cheat you and then wait for more."

This expectation of financial aid from one returned from the United States was encouraged by custom and tradition. America was the land of gold. He who returned was expected, or made to believe that he was obligated, to share some of his good fortune with the less fortunate members of his family. The psychology of emigration was based on this kind of reasoning, which was fostered by newspapers, periodicals, government leaders, and others. The repatriate was considered a family benefactor, or even "a saviour." Some of the earlier arrivals were quite generous, and the practice spread until it became traditional for villagers and relatives to expect aid. Nor could one lose sight of the poverty of the people. They were poor, they did need help, and they looked for assistance to those who they believed could give it.[8]

Sometimes the ostentatious spending habits and the boastful talk of the returned immigrant encouraged the villagers to solicit help from him. The Greek-American might talk about the wages he earned, the profits he reaped in his business, or the extent of his property holdings in the United States. Such verbal displays might be prompted by the repatriate's desire to win an attractive young maiden as a wife, by his sense of self-importance, or perhaps by his pent-up spending powers. This was a second adolescence. The bumptious returnee could be compared with the youngster who saved during the year in order to spend when the circus came to town. Eccentric vocal and spending habits convinced many villagers that the Greek-American was precisely the kind of person they were looking for to help them out of their difficulties. What the villagers often failed to realize was that these were the abnormal, pretentious spending habits of people who had worked and saved in order to splurge on just such an occasion.

Solicitous relatives, anxious to make the visit of a brother or a cousin a pleasant one, took precautions to prevent a repetition of the unhappy experiences that had made many regret their return to Greece. One intelligent Greek who had himself spent a few years in the United States told of the careful preparations he made to receive his brother when the latter came home for a visit:

My brother left Greece at the age of twelve and returned at the age of fifty-seven. He spent forty-two years in the United States. He had a non-Greek wife who passed away and he was finding it difficult to adjust himself after her death.

After some persuading I got him to come to Greece, hoping he would remain permanently. I went to Pireaus to meet him when his ship arrived. I wanted to help him through his most difficult period. The first few weeks were hard. Here was this fifty-seven-year-old man—shocked by what he saw. I knew that life was going to be hard for him in the beginning. I was in the United States six years and I remember my troubles.

I tried to ease the transition for him. I told him to give what money he had to give to relatives and stop there. The fondness of relatives for Greek-Americans is limitless. So are their demands. That is why they treat them like "long-lost brothers."

I arranged to rent a good, clean room for him while he stayed in Athens. I bought good meats, butter, foodstuffs, and even stocked him with choice American toilet tissue. But my brother was unhappy. He missed his ham and eggs for breakfast, his toast, butter, and jelly. What I tried to do for him was a poor substitute for what he had in America. The food didn't please him. The lack of conveniences and the manners of the people infuriated him. He was annoyed because he couldn't have his clothes cleaned and pressed as quickly as he could in the United States.

We also arranged our village home very neatly but this was of no use. He complained about the lack of plumbing and toilets in the village. At one point I asked him if he remembered how he lived before he left for the United States. But he didn't seem to remember much. If he knew once, he must have forgotten. What would have pleased him years ago didn't please him now.

The problems of adjusting to village life varied from person to person; some made the adjustment with a minimum of difficulty, while others underwent the most trying experiences. Many led a peculiar life from the start. After the first two or three months they felt frustrated. No longer did they enjoy being in Greece. They grew tired of doing nothing, of a life that seemed unimportant and purposeless. "When one has seen a better life he knows it and feels it when he is without it." Some became discouraged and left for the United States, or else moved to a city; others reconciled themselves to the inevitable, threw themselves into the customary manual labor and became an integral part of the rural community, but without the enthusiasm they had brought with them from the United States. They reverted to type in much the same way as the Greek-Americans who had been in America from 1907 to 1923, working in the lumber mills of Oregon and Washington. After the return to Greece, these workers used the primitive lumbering methods of their compatriots despite their years of experience in a modern lumber camp.

A few unfortunates neither left the village nor became a part of it. They found fault with everything, and lived on memories of the past. They spent years resisting assimilation, until one day they simply forgot that they were different from the rest. Eventually little remained to distinguish them from other villagers except the investments they had made, and perhaps some of the external evidences of their having lived in the United States. They lost their ambitions because they could not find an outlet for their energies; after the first gifts to relatives, the purchase of land, and the building of homes, they were unable to accomplish much. Such individuals would have been happier, and their villages would have profited, had outlets been found for their capital and energies.⁹

It was not only in the villages that Greek-Americans suffered unhappy or disillusioning experiences, for many repatriates who settled in the cities and larger towns also found life discouraging. Besides warding off demanding relatives, feeling annoyed by the lack of conveniences, and finding the food unpalatable, they complained about the deceptive practices of the local merchants. In the United States they had grown accustomed to paying a marked price and trusting to the integrity of the merchant to deliver the goods for which they had bargained. But in Greece marked prices were rare, and haggling at the counter was common. Purchasers were not always sure they would get what they had purchased, but had to be on guard against short measure, inferior merchandise, diluted goods, and other tricks of the trade employed by the unethical. Repatriates often blasted out indiscriminately against all Greek merchants, much to the annoyance of those who dealt fairly with their patrons. Easily forgotten were the sharp practices that prevailed in the United States, possibly because they were more subtle. In Greece the Greek-Americans expected the local merchants to deal honestly with them.

The prevalence of sharp trading practices in a Balkan country such as Greece was not to be denied. The country was small and poverty-stricken, suffering from invasions, weak governments, economic crises, dependence on foreign powers, and periodically from heavy influxes of refugees. Faith in banks and bankers, and confidence in the political leadership of the nation were lacking. Economic security was unknown to the masses, and the Greeks had long since developed a philosophy of being the poorest among the poor. In truth, the Greeks could hardly afford to relax. The crafty ones kept what funds they had under tight control, not knowing when the next crisis was going to strike; they also tried to extract all they could from those who they believed "had it" and from others too. For such people the returned immigrants proved an easy mark. "They were like children in handling money," remarked one nomarch. Some Greeks operated on the theory that money was easily earned in the United States, and that the repatriates had more than they needed.

The matrimonial position of the returning immigrant who happened to be a bachelor was much more satisfactory than the financial picture. In fact, such a person was in an enviable position in Greece. In the village, he was among the most eligible of the males. Advanced years were not always a handicap, because in the eyes of the most desperate families the financial security of the Greek-American adequately compensated for any lack of youth. Also the word had spread that in the United States potential husbands asked for wives instead of dowries, and marriageable girls and their families hoped that the returned villager was sufficiently Americanized to do likewise. This furnished a golden opportunity for the repatriate who preferred a wife of his own nationality and from his own village, and for the father who was too poor to provide a dowry for his daughter.[10]

Among the repatriates who were married after their return to Greece, reactions to the dowry system varied. Some Greek-Americans freely admitted that they had benefited from the system. One said, "I received a dowry when I was married. I got a home in Patras and some money and clothes, furniture, utensils, etc. I did well." Another residing in Larissa also confessed that he had received a substantial dowry when he married a local girl. On the other hand, contrary views were often expressed. Explained one observer: "In my opinion a dowry was not demanded by the returned Greeks. The Greek-Americans considered it a disgrace to expect money or an inheritance from a wife. These people emphasized the family of the bride and not the money." This was confirmed by a Greek-American: "I didn't get a *preeka* [dowry] when I returned to get married. But in Greece this is important. Most Greeks returning from the United States didn't think of asking for a *preeka*. In the United States you marry a person for what he is and not for what he has."

The repatriated immigrant from the United States did not always break down the dowry system in Greece, but he was much more likely to do so than a person who had not been to America. If the age disparities in some of these marriages are overlooked, which is sometimes difficult, the marrying Greek-Americans helped to bring economic democracy to the altar.

CHAPTER FOUR

ECONOMIC FORTUNES AND MISFORTUNES

AFTER THE First World War many Greek-Americans repatriated themselves with the intention of resuming life as farmers, but on a more extensive scale than before their departure. Those who established themselves in the cities planned to buy at least one house, often more; if they bought more than the one to be used as a home, the others were to serve as income-yielding property. Some expected to acquire apartment buildings or to enter into mercantile pursuits. Others purchased raincoats, shoes, sugar, or other goods in the United States which they hoped to sell for a profit on a rising Greek market. A few believed they might serve as representatives for American business firms in Greece, or perhaps establish businesses based on their experiences in the United States. Booster Greek-American publications, moved by an unbridled spirit of Panhellenism, portrayed the homeland as an excellent prospective market for steel, automobiles, farming equipment, refrigerators, and textiles, and even as the future industrial center of the Near East.[1]

Meanwhile, the supernationalists in Greece kept their eyes firmly fixed on the imperial dream—the incorporation of Constantinople and large segments of Asia Minor into a Greater Greece and the revival of the glories of the Byzantine Empire. Thousands of Greek-Americans who voluntarily repatriated themselves were fully aware of the military aims of the mother

---

[1] For notes to chap. 4, see pp. 143–144.

country, as were the many others who, forced to leave homes in various countries, also went back to Greece. As for the latter, "The Russian revolution started [their] home-coming movement with the exodus... from Odessa, the Crimea, other parts of the Black Sea coast, the Southern Ukraine, the Kouban and the Caucasus." Greek immigrants in the United States, and repatriates with the money they brought from America, pumped millions of dollars into the inflated economy of the ambitious little nation.[2] The head of the National Bank of Greece breathed an air of optimism, shared by many others, when he hopefully reminded his compatriots that Greek troops were at the portals of Constantinople. "The whole Nation is willingly submitting itself to every sacrifice for obtaining sanction and respect for the rights of Hellenism...."[3]

The repatriates, either voluntary or involuntary, who expected to live in a Greater Greece were disappointed, especially those coming from the United States. The endless feuding among rival political factions, the mismanagement of the Greek military campaign in Asia Minor, and the first forced internal loan together created an unhappy state of affairs. The first forced loan floated by the Greek government on April 7, 1922, to help supply its armed forces, called for 1,600,000,000 drachmas. "Bank notes of 5, 10, 25, 100, 500, and 1,000 drachmas were cut... in half; the half bearing the picture of the founder of the National Bank of Greece [George Stavros] was to be declared legal tender at one half the value of the whole note, while the Government would hold the other half of the note bearing the crown, this latter half to be replaced by bonds." The bonds paid 6½ per cent interest and were to fall due in 20 years.[4] Although foreigners in Greece were exempt from the forced loan, the Greek government requested the United States Legation in Athens to help avert fraud on the part of its citizens by passing upon "the amounts and designations in the possession of every American in Greece... of bank notes,... deposits, ... and... debts owed by Greeks to Americans and falling due within the next three months...."[5]

The forced loan influenced the numerous Greek-Americans

who had converted their dollars into drachmas, and others who had thought of repatriating themselves. Most repatriates were subject to the terms of the loan because they had failed to become United States citizens; even if they had, it is doubtful that they would have been exempt from the operations of the law. Some repatriates, apparently believing they could escape the loan, tried to establish their status as citizens of the United States. The case of one "C. S." in 1922 illustrates this approach and also reveals the position of the United States Legation in such matters. "C. S." had emigrated to America in 1888, become a United States citizen in Galveston, Texas, in 1895, and returned to Greece in 1919, presumably for a visit with his family. In acting upon his petition, an American consular official wrote:

> The affiant has been residing in Greece for the past three years and this is the first time during that period that he has made an attempt to secure recognition of his status as an American citizen. Owing to the fact that so many Americans of Greek origin are now endeavoring to secure such recognition in order to escape payment of the Greek Internal Loan, it is respectfully recommended that the Department refuse to accord further recognition to the affiant and that he be presumed to have expatriated himself.[6]

The complaints resulting from the forced loan were legion. Foreign depositors, especially Greek-Americans in the United States who had large sums in Greek banks, protested loudly and persistently. Those who were United States citizens were theoretically exempt from the provisions of the law, but the many who had not been naturalized were technically subject to its provisions. Meanwhile, the Greek government tried to assure its citizens that the forced loan was a necessary and patriotic expedient for which they would be fully compensated. But the Greek-Americans lost faith in the promises of the Greek government, and responded accordingly. "A large part of the emigrants' savings, which were formerly remitted to their families or deposited with Greek banks, [were] now deposited in banks abroad."[7]

Equally objectionable was the Greek capital tax levy on

movable and immovable property which went into effect on April 1, 1923. By its provisions, property valued up to 50,000 drachmas was exempt from the tax; thereafter a graduated tax was imposed, ranging from 2 per cent on property valued from 50,000 to 100,000 drachmas up to 20 per cent on property appraised at more than 25,000,000 drachmas. The par value of the drachma was 19.3 cents, but the current rate of exchange was about 1 cent. In terms of American money, therefore, property valued up to $5,000 was exempt from the levy, and the maximum 20 per cent was levied on property worth $250,000 or more.[8]

A second forced loan was suddenly floated in 1926, shortly after General T. H. Pangalos had become the virtual dictator of Greece. The Pangalos loan, one of the less novel of a series of measures ranging from a law taxing tourists to a decree stipulating "that ladies' skirts not be more than fourteen inches from the ground," infuriated Greek-Americans as well as others; but it aroused less interest among Europeans who were more curious about the law prescribing the legal length of a woman's skirt. This time the forced loan was for 1,250,000,000 drachmas, bearing 6 per cent interest and payable in 20 years. Current notes above 25 drachmas were cut to reduce their value by 25 per cent. It was reported that this time foreigners would be subject to the loan and that the money would be used for civilian instead of military purposes.[9]

Also disconcerting to the moneylending Greek-American were the debt- and interest-scaling decrees of General John Metaxas, who became dictator of Greece in 1936. Many repatriates lent money at interest rates of 12 and 13 per cent or more. A series of drastic reforms were inaugurated. A moratorium was declared on small debts, sizable debts were sharply reduced, and interest rates were forced down. Welcome as these measures might have been to the debt-ridden peasants, the moneylending classes, including many Greek-Americans, found in them an additional cause for unhappiness.[10]

These fiscal measures forced Greek-Americans who had contemplated the investment of American earnings in their native country to reconsider their plans. Faith in the government of the mother country and its currency was waning; no longer did the repatriates see their native land in the same favorable light as before. Hence capital that once was pumped into the marginal Greek economy was now diverted into other channels. It was unfortunate for Greece that "This source of wealth [was] ... drying up owing to the gradual Americanization of the emigrants, their distrust of the laws passed in Greece concerning bank deposits in foreign currencies, the depreciation of the drachma, and the lack of concern shown by the Greek government for the organization and support of Greek culture in America and for encouraging the repatriation of emigrants."[11]

The repatriates who did invest their money in Greece chose a wide variety of enterprises, including rental properties, hotels, and merchant shops of every conceivable type. They became retail butchers, wholesale meat dealers, clothing store operators, building contractors, pottery-shop owners, truckers, coachmen, barbers, tavern keepers, furriers, confectioners, coffeehouse proprietors, large landowners, and moneylenders. Unfortunately, no statistical evidence as to the number of investors and the amount of money they invested is available.

Although precise information is lacking, it is true that the repatriates who acquired small and diversified interests were fairly numerous. Many failed in their endeavors, but there were plenty of others who won success in their chosen fields. In 1952, three well-established repatriates headed widely divergent but profitable enterprises in Athens. One had invested in a travel agency and a department store that netted him handsome profits; the second headed the largest modern dairy establishment in the country; and the third claimed that he and his brothers had built the first hotel in Greece with modern conveniences. A Greek-American who had settled in Navpaktos, a small town northeast of Patras and the site of historic Lepanto, replied to a question about his business: "I have an interest in threshing machines, a bus, own houses in Athens and Navpaktos, and also have about ten *stremmata* [acres] of orange, lemon, and grapefruit trees." A former Chicagoan said, "When

FORTUNES AND MISFORTUNES

I returned in 1926 I brought thirty-two or thirty-three thousand dollars to Greece.... I bought two houses and the rest I lent out at interest. During the late nineteen-twenties and early nineteen-thirties I had an income of about fifteen thousand drachmas a month." A less successful individual who also returned in 1926 likewise invested his money in a small, three-apartment building which netted him 3,000 drachmas a month. He supplemented this with earnings from a coffeehouse he managed.

Evidences of the fortunes of the repatriates were found in all parts of Greece. Greek-Americans owned some of the largest apartment houses in Salonika; in fact their money helped to rebuild the city during the 1920's. Numerous Peloponnesian villages were inhabited by repatriates who were among the largest landowners in the area. By western standards, the Peloponnesus was extremely poor, but Greeks frequently cited the benefits this historic region gained from its repatriated and expatriated sons.

The fortunes of repatriates in the Dodecanese Islands were comparable to those on the Greek mainland. One who returned to the island of Rhodes in 1930 earned a meager living from fishing and from guiding tourists in Lindos. A more prosperous repatriate was in the hotel business with two brothers-in-law, one an Egyptian-Greek and the other a Greek-American. A former steelworker and sponge diver from Tarpon Springs, Florida, operated a small fruit stand in the central market place of the city of Rhodes. In nearby Kremasti lived scores of Greek-Americans whose savings had converted their village into one of the most prosperous on the island. A number of Greek-Americans were located on the island of Karpathos, another of the Dodecanese group; estimates placed the number who had emigrated to the United States from the island at about five thousand. Many returned to Karpathos with sums ranging from $10,000 to $20,000, enough to buy a house, some land, and animals, or to acquire a small business.[12]

Immigrants who became professional men in the United States and then repatriated themselves were few in number.

Several engineers, however, were comfortably established in Greece before the Second World War. "I was in the construction business during the early years of my arrival," said one. "I also deposited a thousand dollars in a Greek bank." Another engineer, apparently of some professional stature, replied, "I was in good economic shape before the war."

Establishing himself in business often proved a difficult adjustment for the Greek-American, after having lived in the United States where western standards prevailed. If the repatriate had been away for many years, he would be unfamiliar with local commercial methods and the psychology of the people. He might also seem a stranger, or even a foreigner, to most of the people in a country where economic opportunities were limited and where it was customary to deal with acquaintances or relatives. The immediate members of the repatriate's family, his close friends and relatives, were the only people who really knew him; and he needed a personal following in many instances in order to launch a profitable business.

Business methods in Greece caused the entrepreneur endless trouble. The misguided relative, the schemer, the promoter, and the sharpster often were a source of irritation to the naïve. Said one Greek-American: "The people are tricky, shifty, and sharp at trading." Eliot G. Mears, an authority on Near Eastern commercial methods, was more restrained in his appraisal: "Business methods in Greece today [1929] are distinctive. Judged by western standards, they fail to meet some tests of good practice. It is not surprising, therefore, that there are many business firms in foreign countries which have had one or more experiences of an unpleasant character with Greek firms...." Mears also said that it was refugees from Anatolia and Constantinople who "brought to Greece the commercial traditions of Asia Minor."[12]

One successfully established Greek-American described the problems of adjustment as follows:

One has to labor and manage differently.... The laws are different. A person experiences much agony until he adapts himself to the local scene.

FORTUNES AND MISFORTUNES

Greek patrons are more demanding and complain a lot. It is very difficult to collect debts in Greece. But in some respects the ethics are higher. You need cash to begin a business. Starting on a credit basis is almost unknown. Because of this, "fake bankruptcies" never take place in Greece.

The labor laws are different. It is hard to discharge an employee without fear of being sued.

Numerous stories of business failures circulated in Greece, where the margin of permissible error was smaller than in the United States. Many of those who failed were poor business managers to begin with, inexperienced in the field which they entered, and they would probably have been unsuccessful in the United States under the same competitive conditions. A Cretan who spent twenty-one years in America possibly spoke for many other failures when he said: "I gave my customers too much credit and was unable to collect." Unfamiliarity with Greek laws, customs, and traditions prompted some Greek-Americans to conclude that an immigrant who spent some years in the United States had thereby unsuited himself for a business career in Greece. Hindsight taught many repatriates that they should have proceeded cautiously and should have kept reserve funds in the United States where their money would have been more secure.

The Second World War had devastating effects on the economic fortunes of the Greek-Americans, as it did on the majority of the Greek population. To some it brought complete ruination, and to thousands of others a drastic whittling down of their resources. The outbreak of war in 1940 also disarranged the lives of an undisclosed number of Greek-Americans who were visiting in Greece and found it impossible to return to the United States. But once hostilities ceased in 1945, the visitors were given the opportunity to leave for America as soon as provisions for their embarkation could be arranged.

One repatriate after another told how the war, bank failures, inflation, civil strife, defaulting debtors, and rent controls ruined him. "When the war came I was cleaned out," said one. "Now I live in one of my houses. The house has three apartments and

I have these rented. But they are under rent control. Before the war I got 10,000 drachmas a month which was very good.... Now I get about 480,000 to 500,000 drachmas which is poor.... I also have lost my bank savings and what money I lent out to borrowers." A Greek-American who had once felt reasonably secure said: "I lost everything I had in the bank at the time of the occupation." A small property owner also stated: "Before the war I got 3,000 drachmas a month. This paid me well. Now I get 138,000 drachmas. This is nothing. During the Nazi occupation I lost my place of business—a coffeehouse." A small butcher-shop operator claimed a similar fate: "The war, the occupation, and the guerrillas wiped me out."

The year 1940 was the great dividing line in the fortunes of many Greek-Americans. An American-trained engineer remarked: "I was in good economic shape in 1940. By 1945 I was just like the college student when he graduates." Substantially the same story came from another: "I was well off before 1940—a pasha. I collected rent and interest on loans and I also had a business." A heated Greek-American protested bitterly about the effects of Greece's wartime controls: "Rent controls have hurt most of us who have invested our money in income-yielding property. They should be abolished.... I would be in bad shape if it wasn't for the veteran benefits I received from the United States government." Another who repatriated himself during the Great Depression spent what little money he had on hospital and doctor bills. During the war his plight became so acute that he sold the gold in his teeth for a little food. A small hotel manager who had invested his money in his business said, "When the Germans came they took my beds, furniture. I lost everything."

The misfortunes of many repatriates were summed up as follows: "Many who had a little money aided relatives and friends in distress.... Others proved to be poor managers of what business or property they had. Many invested their money in income-yielding property which they expected to provide for them for the rest of their days. The war, the occupation, and the guerrillas came along and caused additional hardship. Rent controls were imposed. The investments of these Greek-Americans failed to bring the returns to which they were accustomed before the war."

The repatriates fared reasonably well before the Second World War, especially those who had invested in homes and other real estate. Those who had deposited money in banks often lost it. Frequently, Greek-Americans had more to lose from the war and its aftermath than ordinary Greeks who had never left the country. That is why many protested as loudly as they did.

An American veteran of the First World War, who had suffered reverses, explained that later repatriates were much shrewder in handling their savings and investments than his generation had been. They profited from the tragic experiences of the earlier arrivals. "Instead of bringing their savings as we did," he added, "they kept them in the United States where they were much safer...." One of three brothers who returned to a small island in the Aegean Sea said: "Our money is invested in real estate in Detroit. Each of us draws an income of five hundred dollars a month." A Salonika coffeehouse operator who returned in 1933 admitted that he had a substantial sum of money deposited in American banks. He never brought it with him to Greece.

Surprisingly enough, a number of repatriates claimed that their economic fortunes were about the same in Greece as they had been in the United States, and a few even asserted that they were better off financially. A former New York shoeshine parlor operator, who had lost almost all of his savings before he reached Greece, said that he fared better in his native land than in the United States. He attributed this happy outcome to the many skills he had acquired in America. "I have built everything since I returned in 1920 and without funds from the United States." A steamship ticket broker most emphatically stated, "Yes, I am much better off.... I have property. My son operates a department store." Still another added: "I am better off in Greece. I head a big business.... It has about six hundred distributing points in the country." A villager replied: "My economic position is about the same. I invested most of my money in real estate. I didn't lose anything in a Greek bank."

The post-World War II era witnessed the arrival of "social security repatriates"—retired laborers, factory hands, railroad workers, and others covered by the social security system of the United States. Included in this group were some who had once lost hope of repatriating themselves. But New Deal legislation revived these almost extinct aspirations by making it possible to collect social security payments in any part of the world, since there were no citizenship stipulations attached to receipt of the checks. Thus the retired repatriate could rediscover his native land. In fact, social security began to assume global proportions, though most of those receiving payments abroad live in some European country. The amount paid to all recipients living abroad has increased spectacularly since the Second World War, from $1,633,000 in 1947 to approximately $15,800,000 in 1953.[14] (See table 3.)

The Greeks were in the vanguard of the social security repatriates. Restlessness on the part of formerly active employees, combined with the shrinking purchasing power of the dollar in the United States, added a new chapter to the old story of "making money in the States and returning home to spend it." In Greece a social security repatriate could stretch a meager pension into a comfortable livelihood, particularly if he was married, for his wife might qualify to receive half as much as he did. An American correspondent, perhaps exaggerating his point, claimed that the cashing of United States government checks in Greece was becoming a minor industry. "At the central headquarters of several banks in Athens a number of Americans are employed to handle the avalanche of checks."[15]

In 1949, once the civil war had ended, the number of social security and railroad retirement repatriates who went to Greece increased sharply. In 1949 there were 653 such repatriates who received a total of only $195,395; by 1952 the number of recipients had increased to 1,906, and the amount to $1,015,883 (see table 4). But retirement in one's home country had its tragic aspects as well. Some repatriates were in poor physical condition when they reached Greece, and died before they could collect the first check. In 1953 the death rate among social security repatriates was placed at about fifteen per month.

TABLE 3
Old-Age and Survivors' Insurance Paid to Recipients Living Abroad, 1940–1953

Year	Number of recipients	Total amount paid
1940	100	$ 37,000
1941	204	44,000
1942	206	36,000
1943	200	48,000
1944[a]	...	......
1945[a]	...	......
1946[a]	...	......
1947	5,800	1,633,000
1948	8,800	2,328,000
1949	11,038	2,977,000
1950	13,800	6,715,000
1951	18,700	8,790,000
1952	25,104	13,143,000
1953	30,145	15,800,000

[a] Data are not available for these years.
SOURCE: *Analysis of the Social Security System*, Part 2, 83d Cong., 1st sess. (Washington, 1953).

TABLE 4
Railroad Retirement and Social Security Payments in Greece, 1949–1952

Year	Number	Amount
1949	653	$ 195,395
1950	952	343,625
1951	1,413	694,564
1952	1,906	1,015,883

SOURCE: Data made available by the office of the United States Consul-General in Athens.

Closely related to the social security repatriates, in their dependence on the United States government, were veterans of the First World War, many of whom belonged to the American Legion, Department of Greece. Once they constituted the only important group receiving checks from the United States government. Since 1950, however, veterans have been surpassed by social security and railroad retirement recipients both in numbers and in the amount of money received (see table 5).

The veterans of the First World War and the social security repatriates have added in a minor way to the dollar holdings of Greece. Most of these people probably will remain there permanently, and life in the United States will become but a memory, if it has not already done so. "But once a month an envelope will arrive from the United States government and with it the

TABLE 5
Payments to Veterans of the First World War in Greece, 1949–1952

Year	Number	Amount
1949	721	$590,202
1950	782	622,926
1951	801	610,082
1952	833	647,604

Source: Data made available by the office of the United States Consul-General in Athens.

remembrance of a generous country far away which, even to a retired septuagenarian, pays higher wages than many people in the Old World can earn during their active years." Furthermore, the monthly checks will be backed by one of the strongest economies in the world, and will spare the repatriate from having to rely for his sustenance exclusively on the unstable marginal economy of Greece."[16]

A rather novel situation developed in 1952 when a group of 120 repatriated Greek-Americans living on the island of Karpathos, through the aid of an American attorney, declared themselves hardship cases in a letter to the President of the United States, and asked to be included within the provisions of the social security system. It appeared that most of these people had repatriated themselves before the social security program was adopted. Asserting that they had worked hard and that they were now in need of help, they inquired about the possibility of receiving retroactive reimbursement for their labor in the

United States. An informal investigation into the economic status of 92 of the 120 self-proclaimed hardship cases revealed that the majority of the Karpathians were well off financially. Many of them owned land, homes, and small shops, or else were supported by children in the United States. It is true that some were destitute, but the majority fared reasonably well according to Greek standards."[17]

The repatriates' difficulties stemmed in large part from their desire to maintain an American standard of living in Greece, an ideal almost impossible of achievement. Many of the returned immigrants, during their less happy moments, reminisced about the economic opportunities they had forsaken in exchange for the chance to retire in the land of their birth. As things turned out, the price paid for repatriation was often a high one.

CHAPTER FIVE

SOME CASE HISTORIES

The experiences of Greek-Americans, as both immigrants and repatriates, brought humor, drama, tragedy, and success into their lives. To these people, nothing stood out more vividly than their personal histories, and it would be difficult to match the emotional intensity with which the repatriates described what they had experienced. A few of their stories will serve to illustrate the various problems—economic, occupational, personal, social—that made the return to Greece a challenge, and often an adventure.

1. *Honor, Prosperity, and a Beauty Shop*

Mr. G. left Greece as a seaman and landed in New York City in 1921, when rigid bars were being erected against immigrants from southern and eastern Europe. His early years in the United States were like those of other immigrants, except that he proved to be more adaptable than many of his compatriots. He arrived in New York on a Friday, and on the following Monday he enrolled in a beginner's English class. At first, the language problem created difficulties but he soon overcame them.

His immediate concern was to find the means of supporting himself and his parents, who were in Greece. He got one job working eight hours a day in New York to take care of his own needs, and another eight-hour job in Brooklyn to provide for his parents. Thus his early years were marked by long hours of labor, unbalanced living, and dreams of returning to Greece.

Eventually Mr. G. became a hairdresser, a calling that was strange to most immigrants. He was, however, successful in it, and after three and a half years established his own business in a prominent New York hotel. He made money, was happy, and wanted to remain in the United States, but he could not forget that he had a fiancée in Greece. The logical procedure for him was to become an American citizen and arrange for the young woman's voyage to the United States; in fact, he tried to do this but became annoyed over the inevitable delays. His *filotimo* (honor), he said, got the better of him, so he returned to Greece to marry the girl who had waited eight years. Accidentally he had served himself well, for he left the United States with all his money in August, 1929, two months before the stock market crash.

In Greece Mr. G. invested his savings in rental property, which netted him about 10,000 prewar drachmas a month, and in a beauty shop. The other beauty salons in Athens were patterned after European models, but there was none of the kind he established. His shop was built around his American experiences. The novelty of his business made it necessary for him to start from the ground up; he had to train his own help and build his own trade. Training the help caused him the greatest difficulty, for no sooner had he educated an employee to his own ways than the employee left to work for someone else. Mr. G. also had to make the necessary adjustment to Greek business methods and practices, a process that required about two years. In 1939, on a visit to the United States, he purchased supplies and equipment to take back to Greece. By 1940 he had developed what was probably the most modern beauty shop in Athens.

Like many others, Mr. G. spoke enthusiastically about the government of General John Metaxas, prime minister of Greece from 1936 to 1941. By contrast with the aftermath, according to Mr. G., Greece under Metaxas experienced a modern "golden age." Wages were good, and peace, economic stability, and contentment prevailed. Whether the facts would substantiate Mr. G's claims was beside the point; in 1953 he and countless other Greeks looked back longingly to the dictator's regime.

Both of Mr. G's children were educated in American-sponsored colleges in Athens. His son was graduated from Athens College and his daughter attended Pierce College. On the wall of his office was a diploma issued in 1934 by the California School of Beauty Culture, San Francisco, to one of Mr. G.'s employees.

Mr. G. is unlike the average American beautician in his range of interests. He concerns himself with philosophic and ethical topics as well as with beauty culture. He is conversationally at home in discussions on the difference in British and American methods of aiding Greece, on faith and courage in times of crisis, on hard times and ethics, on "the spiritual as well as the mechanical side of man," and on what Greece as a former major civilization can teach the United States to prevent it from disintegrating.

2. Repatriation and Pasteurization

Mr. S. heads the largest dairy firm in Greece. Like other repatriates, he founded his business with dollars and experience earned in America. From his office he has a perfect view of the Acropolis, which stands out vividly in the background.

A Peloponnesian from Arcadia, he came to the United States in 1905 and lived in Chicago. In 1912 he and his brothers formed an ice-cream company as a family concern. That same year he left the United States to fight in the Balkan Wars and returned in 1916. In 1928 he made another of his many trips to Greece, this time to marry a native girl, and again returned to the United States. He repatriated himself in 1934.

In Greece Mr. S. proved an innovator, as well as a successful businessman. His greatest contribution was the pasteurization of milk. The theory of pasteurization had been known in Greece before Mr. S. formed his company, but the capital and the managerial and technical skills needed to put it to practical use

CASE HISTORIES

were lacking. The process thus had to await the proper combination of these various factors before the product could be marketed. Mr. S., possessing the wherewithal and the knowhow, introduced pasteurized milk in 1935 with equipment imported from the United States. A technician from the family firm in Chicago was brought to Greece to teach the process to Greek workers.

The people most receptive to the idea of pasteurized milk proved to be returned Greek-Americans. They knew all about the product and its merits from their stay in the United States. The local milk dealers, however, fought the innovation and even boasted that they would drive the Greek-Americans into the sea, or perhaps send them back to America. At first Mr. S.'s company was looked upon as a foreign firm. When the building was being constructed many people wondered what was going to be housed in it and how long the Greek-Americans would remain in business. Competing distributors misrepresented the pasteurization process and forced the firm to establish milk stations instead of the routes it had planned to introduce. A backlog of American capital helped the company to survive the early opposition and eventually to become the largest firm of its kind in Greece.

According to Mr. S., it took about four months to allay Greek suspicions of pasteurized milk. The process of educating the public was undoubtedly hastened by the support of cattle breeders, animal husbandry experts, and doctors. The change in attitude is evidenced by figures from the company's books: in 1935 it handled about 2,000 gallons of milk a day, but in 1953 from 18,000 to 20,000 gallons. Besides milk, the company distributes yogurt, ice cream, casein, and casein products.

3. "I Wish I Was in Peoria Tonight"

Mr. A. lives in a small Peloponnesian village of 200 inhabitants. He left for the United States in 1921 and returned to his village in 1932, during the depths of the depression. During his stay in America he lived in Peoria, Illinois; Newton, Iowa; Venice, California; and Boston, Massachusetts. He worked in a restaurant, purchased one of his own, and also sold fruit.

Mr. A.'s version of why he returned to Greece differed from that of his two sons. He said that he was unable to bring his family to the United States because of the excessive transportation costs, and because of his failure to become an American citizen. A son, however, said that his father had never planned to bring his family to the United States, and that he had always thought of returning to Greece. Mr. A. would never admit that he had hankered for his native land and, in fact, he often regretted his decision to repatriate himself. He considered himself a fool. His earnings in America had been meager, but he fared worse in Greece, for he had to depend on his small landholdings and on the financial help his sons sent from Athens. If the opportunity to return to the United States were given him, he would leave immediately. He never realized how contented he had been in America until he went to Greece to live. Today America is but a dream, and he tries to capture some of its spirit by glancing through discarded copies of *Life* magazine. When asked for a final comment, Mr. A. responded with the title of a once popular tune: "I Wish I Was in Peoria Tonight."

4. *From Bricks to Baskets*

Mr. M. D. is a small sidewalk merchant in Salonika. He sells baskets. He was born in 1889 in a small village in East Thrace and left for the United States in 1913, right after the First Balkan War, to escape serving in the Turkish army. Before the war, it had been possible to avoid military duty by making a money payment, but this privilege ceased once the fighting broke out. His departure, he said, was aided by a friend in the Russian consulate in Constantinople; Russia in those days exerted great influence in Turkey. When Mr. M. D. reached the consular offices, he discovered that many others were also seeking to escape service in the Turkish army. He sailed from Constantinople for Piraeus on a Russian ship, from Piraeus for Patras on a Greek ship, and from Patras for New York on an

American one. He worked for a brick company in Joliet, Illinois, from 1913 to 1919.

Mr. M. D. would have remained in the United States had it not been for his parents who were refugees in Salonika and whom he wanted to bring to America. On his way to Salonika he stopped briefly in Paris, where he accidentally met a former coworker from the Joliet brick company for which he had worked. Ironically enough, his friend was returning to the United States from Salonika, where he had served with the armed forces, and told Mr. M. D. that the city was in ruins and advised him not to go there. But Mr. M. D., determined to see his parents, ignored this advice. When he reached his destination, he was disappointed to find that Salonika appeared like a village. Worse still, his mission proved fruitless, for his parents did not care to go to the United States. Instead, they wanted him to remain in Greece. When pressures of the most inconceivable types were exerted to prevent his departure, Mr. M. D. decided to remain in Greece.

He had had $3,500 when he reached Greece, the result of six years of labor and saving in the United States. After a few months' vacation, he left for a village in East Thrace where he invested his money in a general store. He managed this until he was compelled to serve in the Greek army, and then his brother took over the management. When the Turks invaded the region and drove out the Greeks, he lost his investment.

Mr. M. D. says that he owes much to the United States. It saved him from serving in the Turkish army and gave him an opportunity to work and save. He acquired good work habits which helped him obtain a fresh start in life once his savings were exhausted. Like many others, he observed that Greeks expect help from those who return from the United States.

5. "I Never Was Happy in the United States"

Mr. G. R. is one of the few middle-aged men who returned to Greece after the Second World War. He was born of Greek parents in a village near the Dardanelles. Unlike most others, he left for the United States in 1932, during the depths of the depression.

Before departing from Greece, Mr. G. R. had an impression that Americans were of three types: the wealthy, the gangsters, and the cowboys. This impression was created by what he had seen in American motion pictures. But when he reached the United States, he discovered that there were poor people too, and that they were not much different from those of Europe.

Mr. G. R. lived in America for eighteen years. He first worked in a restaurant and then, forced to relinquish his original plan of saving and going to school, he established a business of his own. He lived in a small Pennsylvania town and attended national and religious celebrations in a nearby city where there was a Greek colony and church. The fact that he was born in Turkish territory and that he had a good Greek education helped him to preserve his national identity. He admitted, "I never was happy in the United States. My mind was always in Greece."

Mr. G. R. left for Greece with some favorable impressions of the United States. He liked the freedom and independence of the people, the American sense of justice, trial by jury, and the fact that people are not "pushed around." He could travel about the country unmolested by police authorities, buy a car when he wanted to, and enjoy himself. Mr. G. R. observed that the American woman, independent, adaptable, and self-sustaining, is different from the Greek woman. As a rule, Greeks condemn the working girl; they feel that there is something degrading, even immoral, about her working for a living. Greeks marry women of their own nationality because they believe that they make better wives, and also that they preserve cherished customs and traditions.

Mr. G. R. believes that he will never regret his repatriation. Greece offers him fewer opportunities, it is true, but still he feels happier there. He no longer has to contend with exhausting restaurant work, and his health has improved. He makes less money but he does not work so hard. And in Greece he is free of the antiforeign feeling that irked him in America. Greece has

CASE HISTORIES

probably gained from Mr. G. R.'s repatriation. Besides owning his own hotel business, he is of higher mental and social caliber than most repatriates. His two brothers are well established in the electrical supplies business, and enjoy a social position in Greece superior to that held by Mr. G. R. in the United States.

6. "If I Only Had Left My Money to My Brothers and Returned to the United States"

Mr. A. V. P., an Arcadian, lives in constant regret over the mistake he made in returning to Greece. A well-dressed man, he subsists on income from rental property.

Mr. A. V. P. spent twenty-two years in the United States, living in San Francisco and in a small Oregon community. During his first years he worked in a box factory and on a railroad construction gang. Before returning to Greece, he was in the confectionery business. In 1927 he decided to visit his mother in Greece and then return to America. From the sale of his business and property interests he netted $25,000, which he took with him in disregard of his banker's advice.

Once in Greece, Mr. A. V. P. became involved in several situations that made it difficult for him to leave. First, he married a Greek girl. Then he invested unwisely in a business venture that drained him of his liquid capital. The loss made him regret his decision to take his money out of America, but he blamed only himself for his poor judgment.

Mr. A. V. P. has unkind words to say about relatives. They were a big problem when he went home to Greece. "In those early days, few warned you about being on guard against relatives.... Now the returning ones are more careful.... If I only had left my money to my brothers and returned to the United States."

7. The Saga of a Karagiozopechtis

Mr. D. G., aged sixty-nine, lives in a village near Tripolis. Born in 1883, he went to America in 1899 at the age of sixteen. Chicago was his last place of residence in the United States, where his unique experiences took him to many localities. In addition to the fairly ordinary occupations of coachman, coffeehouse proprietor, restaurateur, and saloonkeeper, Mr. D. G. was also a *Karagiozopechtis* (silhouette performer). During his stay in the United States, there were probably not more than five or six such performers staging shows in the Greek colonies.

The coffeehouse customarily served as the stage for such shows. Mr. D. G. said that the method of compensating him for his performances, which ran from one night to one month, was standard. The coffeehouse proprietor usually paid the performer's room rent, and furnished him with coffee and tobacco. If profits from the sale of refreshments were substantial, the manager of the house (the *Kafenji*) usually gave him $20 to have him stay over. But the performer's remuneration came chiefly from patrons, who gave what they pleased during designated breaks in the performance when a tray was passed among them for contributions. A set price of admission was unknown. On a profitable week end Mr. D. G. collected as much as $100, but this good fortune was all too infrequent. Like other performers, he gambled with his money, losing it as quickly as he earned it.

Non-Greeks called the performance of a *Karagiozopechtis* a "Greek show." In such a show the Greeks were portrayed as God-fearing Christians, and the Turks as *Christianomachus*, or the "enemies of the Christians." When the performer appeared in a community with a substantial Turkish element, he reversed the order and portrayed the Turk as the hero and the Greek as the villain. Among the plays performed were *Katsantonis, Captain Gre, Athanasios Diakos, Tsekoureous, Necrazosa*, and *Mysteres*.

In 1913 Mr. D. G. left the United States for Greece, to fight in the Balkan Wars. Although a member of the Panhellenic Union, he paid his own passage. When he arrived in Greece he had only $500 with him, which he spent quickly. His relatives, he said, informed him that he was of no use to them because he didn't bring them any help. He used what little money he had left after the war ended to buy a horse and buggy so that he could earn a living as a coachman in Tripolis. He chose to remain in Greece permanently.

Mr. D. G. is a poor man who relies on his daughter and son-in-law for support, though relatives in Chicago send him clothes periodically. His few material possessions he gained through his stay in America, and he has many times regretted his return to Greece. Like others, he is critical of the Greek's treatment of the Greek-American, but he attributes it to stupidity on the part of the repatriate and to jealousy and envy on the part of those who seek to exploit him. "Lend a person a hundred thousand drachmas and try and collect from him and he calls you a *kounesmenos* [a shaken one]."

8. "I Saw Things I Probably Will Never See Again"

Mr. C. P. was born in a village near Navpaktos, not far from Patras. He left for the United States in 1907 and returned to fight in the Balkan Wars of 1912–1913. He remained in Greece until 1915 and then returned to America. He lived in Philadelphia, Niagara Falls, and Buffalo. In 1920 he repatriated himself, blaming much of his restlessness on ill health.

Mr. C. P. invested several thousand dollars in shoes, which he believed he could sell in Greece at a profit. Once he had thought of buying sugar but a friend dissuaded him. He had reason to regret his choice, for misfortune faced him when some of the shoes were lost in transit across the ocean, others were damaged, and the insurance he carried was insufficient to cover his losses. And even the shoes that did reach their destination did not appeal to Greek women who, unaccustomed to American styles, preferred the low, broad-toed shoe to the high-top, pointed one he had to offer. Mr. C. P. had never been in the shoe business before, hence he knew little about the market.

Upon his return to Greece, Mr. C. P. was mustered into the army and served in the home guards. After his discharge he began life anew. What he had acquired in the way of an estate since his return from the United States he invested in construction materials, two gasoline stations, automobile accessories, and a home. He liked the climate of Greece better than that of the United States, and he was happier in his native land. His greatest fear was over the outbreak of another war.

Mr. C. P.'s experiences and observations were similar to those of other repatriates. When he returned in 1920, he lived with an uncle who helped him find a bride. The uncle expected some financial assistance, which Mr. C. P. felt obliged to give him. The country was retarded, and the people were poor and simple. Poor roads and communications left him with a feeling of isolation. He missed the conveniences in the United States and the systematic way in which the American people went about their work. He complained that Greek-Americans fell victims to scheming villagers and city people who either swindled or overcharged them. The returned immigrants were generous, trusting, and humanitarian; they also considered themselves better than the rest, and he believed they were. He said that the United States gave him *morphosis* (education) and an appreciation of good work habits. "I saw things I probably will never see again."

9. *"I Came to Fight for My Country, Its National Ideals and Aspirations"*

Mr. T. B. is a short-statured, fiery Greek nationalist who leaves little doubt about his devotion to Greece. A Messenian, born in 1889, he emigrated to the United States in 1908. He made two return trips to Greece before he finally repatriated himself. The first was in 1909, when he took a military officer's examination, and the second in 1912, when he went back to fight in the Balkan Wars. Immediately after his final trip to Greece, in 1915, he went into the army.

Mr. T. B. is a loquacious individual, whose remarks in response to questions were lengthy, rhetorical, and passionate. He orated as though he were addressing a great throng in the market place. In his mind the spiritual superiority of Greece was beyond dispute, but he did agree that Greece economically had less to offer than the United States. For example, he had denied himself opportunities for self-advancement by returning to Greece. He also liked the spirit of good will that prevailed in America, the spirit that made one person happy to see another succeed. But he was glad to return and serve his country.

In 1953 the question of extending, curtailing, or eliminating United States aid to Greece concerned him, as it concerned many others. And he found occasion to express his feelings. In effect he said: "The Americans talk about cutting out aid for Greece. They can afford to continue it, and we know we need and deserve it. But if it is eliminated we will survive; we know how to take care of ourselves. We have done it before. We have taken to the hills and have eaten greens and grasses, and we can do it again if we have to. But I would like to see what the Americans will be able to do, if they ever become as desperate and poverty-stricken as the Greeks. Yes, my friend, I would like to see what you will be able to do when you are deprived of your malted milks, your hamburgers, and your apple pies. We have defended ourselves and know how to do it again if we have to, but will you be able to do the same under similar circumstances?"

10. "I Left God's Country to Come to the Devil's"

Mr. S. G. was born in Constantinople in 1900, left for the United States in 1914, and departed for Greece in 1923. Thus his stay in America covered nine years, from age fourteen to age twenty-three. He lived in Pittsburgh, New York City, Akron, Philadelphia, and Baltimore. He worked as an electrician, an elevator boy, a cook, and finally as a chef. He served with the United States Transport Service from 1916 to 1922, making many trips across the ocean with American troops. Once he served as a steward aboard the *Leviathan*.

In 1923 Mr. S. G. decided to visit his folks in Greece. When he arrived, he was welcomed as a person who came from "a civilized society." There was much wining and dining. Only a few asked him for help, since his relatives and parents fortunately were not in want. Despite the advice of his parents, and against his own better judgment, he finally decided to remain in Greece.

With the $3,000 that Mr. S. G. had brought to Greece with him, he first established a chandler's office in the hope that he could do a thriving business supplying American ships. This proved to be a mistake. He then entered the automobile service business in Salonika, but it also ended in failure. He was unable to compete with local Greeks by using American methods. The prevailing code of ethics was something to which he could not reconcile himself. In the end he lost his small capital.

Feeling sufficiently punished for his mistake in coming to Greece to live, he wanted to return to the United States. He said that the Greeks were chronically discontented, and he was among the malcontents. His unhappiness was the deeper because, having been to the United States, he now realized that he had had opportunities and a sense of security there that he finds hard to forget. "I left God's country to come to the devil's." To him America symbolized honesty, decency, and truth. "The American flag is always displayed in my home and will continue to be shown as long as I live."

He wonders whether American immigration laws will ever be relaxed so that those who once lived in the United States can reënter the country. He believes that people like himself, who would be a constructive force in America, should be placed in a category separate from the quota system. As one who knew America, he would do everything in his power to show appreciation for the opportunity to return. He wants to start life anew, to live the remaining years of his life in the United States, die there, and have the satisfaction of knowing he would be buried in peace.

11. "I Planned to Stay in Greece Five or Six Months"

Mr. A. M. was born in Iera Petra (Sacred Rock), Crete, in 1900 and left for the United States in 1912. He lived in Boston for eighteen years and in Concord, New Hampshire, for three. He worked first as a bus boy, then became a chef and pastry cook,

CASE HISTORIES

and finally bought his own restaurant. Upon his return to Greece in 1933, he had to pay 11,000 drachmas because he had failed to render the required military service.

Mr. A. M.'s return to Greece was, he claimed, accidental. He met an acquaintance who was going to Greece, and on the spur of the moment decided to go along. "I planned to stay in Greece five or six months. But within that time I was married." Although Mr. A. M. had never become an American citizen, he wanted to go back to the United States to live. In 1932 he tried to reënter on a forged passport. But at Le Havre, France, he was seized by the authorities and returned to Greece, an unhappy man—frustrated and minus the $320 he paid the schemer for his illicit advice.

In Crete, where Mr. A. M. finally returned to live, his economic experiences were unspectacular. He brought $10,000 with him, leaving about $2,000 on deposit in an American bank. He invested his money in real estate, a grocery store, and a tavern. He fared poorly in the business ventures but, living in one of the houses he had purchased, he derived a small income from the other and from two small farms that he rented on a share basis.

12. *"This Craze for Business and Profits Left Me No Time to Live"*

Mr. P. was the owner of an outdoor cafe located on a high hill overlooking Mytilene Bay, in clear sight of the coast of Asia Minor. Mr. P. had lived in the United States from 1919 to 1940, and had owned a combination restaurant and bar in Albany, New York. He made a lot of money, but only by working hard and by being constantly on the job. "You had to be there if you wanted to make money. You couldn't trust your employees. At the age of thirty-five I had one hundred and fifty thousand dollars. I gave the best years of my life to the United States and I will always remember this. This craze for business and profits left me no time to live. From 1930 to 1940 I made nine trips to Greece, to try and decide where I would live permanently. I had a hard time making up my mind. I was in Greece in 1940 when the war broke out and I couldn't return to the United States. This settled my problem." But he added that in several respects life in Greece was better than it had been in the United States. "One doesn't work as hard. One doesn't have to rush. No matter how poor a person is, he can always find something to eat. Here people understand you better, talk your language."

Mr. P.'s experiences in the United States had some bearing on his future life in Greece. As he said, "In the United States one could do any kind of work. In Greece certain types are unacceptable. You can't do this kind of work, even if you need the job and it is available to you. Because I have been to the United States and have owned a coffeehouse, it is a disgrace for me to put on an apron and wash dishes and I have to hire someone else to do this for me. In the United States I could do this and no one would notice it. But in Greece this is socially unacceptable."

Like others, Mr. P. suffered during the Nazi occupation of Greece. He was arrested, according to his story, with many others on charges of spying for the Allies. Of the fifty-six Greeks who were to be executed, he was one of the six who through sheer fortune managed to escape. "Many Greek-Americans," he added, "aided the Allies, but what good was this to them? The Nazis caught and executed them. If they escaped, they were no better off because the British didn't do anything for them personally."

CHAPTER SIX

THE REPATRIATED AND THEIR CRITICS

The Greek who had spent a number of years in the United States inevitably saw his native land from a different perspective than the Greek who had never been away. The repatriate was fully aware of the distinction, and seldom permitted himself or anyone else to forget it. On various occasions, moreover, he drew sharp comparisons between the ethics of the two countries, the ways of doing business, and the behavior of the people. Such comparisons generally cast Greece in an unfavorable light.

Frustration was all too easily induced in the returned immigrant. Losses suffered through personal business reverses, forced government loans, inability to recover money advanced to friends and relatives, and other unhappy experiences made the repatriate a disgruntled, hypercritical, and sometimes an irrational person. He found fault with the Greek government, with his compatriots, and with those he believed responsible for his misfortunes. He was frequently disinclined to blame himself for poor judgment or unbusinesslike methods, or for his inexperience in dealing with an underprivileged people. It became common practice for the repatriate to dwell on the "lazy men" who congregated in coffeehouses at all hours of the day, to deplore the tendency of the cunning to "live by their wits." If such conditions were tolerable when the repatriate first reached Greece, they speedily became intolerable when his assets and his patience diminished.

REPATRIATED AND THEIR CRITICS

A frustrated Greek-American found psychological gratification in branding Greece a wretched and hopeless land and in dubbing its government leaders incompetent self-seekers. A government official was frequently criticized as a *faga* or "big-eater," and public servants collectively were called *fagades* or "big-eaters." In the critic's opinion, such officials lacked humility and integrity, a failing they evidenced by the practice of nepotism. The average person had no access to a ranking official or, for that matter, to anyone holding even a minor government post. How different this was, remarked one repatriate, from America where it was possible for a simple peanut vendor to shake hands with the President of the United States. Greek-Americans viewed American public servants as loyal, devoted, and conscientious individuals who felt a sense of responsibility to their nation. Although the validity of these views might be subject to debate, it is beyond dispute that they were held by many Greeks, even by some of those who had never been to America. The Greek-Americans had no monopoly on this kind of thinking.

The losses that Greek-Americans suffered from bank failures made them suspicious of the financial institutions of Greece. Many recalled bitterly that in 1922 they had lent half, and in 1926 one-fourth, of their deposits to the Greek government, expecting to be repaid. The government's failure to meet its obligations caused them to lose faith in banks, in Greek currency, and in any future promises the government might make. Consequently Greek-Americans, like the more canny Greeks, began to convert their personal savings into English gold sovereigns, and kept them close at hand. They had greater confidence in the sovereign than in the drachma. Meanwhile, many recalled that they had deposited their savings in American banks with assurance. Except for those who returned after 1933, most repatriated immigrants escaped the ill effects of the Great Depression of 1929–1933, the financial holocaust that wiped out the funds of many depositors.

The repatriates who owned small retail or wholesale shops made no secret of their preference for the American as against the Greek way of transacting business. A businessman accustomed to western commercial methods was distinctly at a disadvantage in competing with local merchants skilled in Levantine ways of trade. There were, of course, some observers who discounted charges that the merchant classes were guilty of unethical practices. Perhaps the Greeks were cruder, or possibly completely lacking in the subtleties of the trade, but they were certainly no more unethical than members of other nationality groups. It was a wonder, the argument went, that the people, after experiencing a series of wars and of political and economic upheavals, retained any moral and ethical values at all.

Many repatriates incurred the wrath of their fellow citizens by complaining of the lack of progress in Greece. A Greek attorney reported an instance of this kind of criticism: "One Greek-American asked me if there wasn't some law in Greece requiring seats to be provided in a public building when a certain number of people entered it, or one governing the safety of the building." The lawyer replied that "there might be such laws in the United States but there aren't any in Greece." Another Greek said that his brother, after an absence of many years, asked the question, "Why hasn't the river near our village been harnessed and a hydroelectric project built?" A prospective repatriate, when visiting his native village in Crete, was shocked by what he saw; he described the community as more retarded than it had been years ago, when he left for the United States. He build an outhouse for his own private use, hoping that the villagers would also acquire the habit of using it. But to no avail; they were suspicious and kept away from it.

The more understanding repatriate, though willing to concede the existence of many of the conditions about which the less tolerant complained, reasoned that such defects had to be accepted as a matter of course once a Greek-American had decided to live in Greece. A repatriate had to forget his American ways; if he prized them above the Greek ways, and was unwilling to compromise, he should have remained in the United States. It was unjust to compare Greece, a Balkan nation, aged, ravaged by wars, military occupations, and poverty, with the United States, a young, western power with wealth and influence. The comparison was ridiculous. Why contrast the two? Why condemn all Greeks and emphasize the unfavorable aspects of Greek society? Former "goatherds" who went off to America and then returning spoke with irreverence about a country whose people had endured much hardship were quite naturally resented. What about the courage, the sacrifices, and the sturdy independent character of the Greeks who had helped to keep the nation alive when other forces tended to tear it asunder?

Stories of dissatisfaction among repatriates circulated widely, and spread the fear that the ties between the people of Greece and Greek-Americans in the United States would be dissolved. It is small wonder that one journalist pleaded with Greeks living abroad: "Do not lose faith in our country. Do not lose your enthusiasm and become discouraged because of what you have seen in various circles. They are clouds that will pass on.... The working Greek population with the aid of those living abroad will see that it isn't true that in Greece all has set except the sun."[1]

How were the repatriates, themselves so critical of Greece, treated by their compatriots? As noted above, early reactions toward them varied from sympathy and respect to contempt and ridicule. Villagers and small-town people were inclined to be less critical, whereas better-educated Greeks and members of cafe society tended to be condescending.

A member of the professional classes, the son of a repatriated Greek-American, stated emphatically: "The immigrants and the returned ones are respected in the provinces. The attitudes of the Athenians should be discounted as those of people who want something for themselves. Look at the bridges, churches, roads, schools, and other public improvements. These people instill something in the village." A member of the Greek Parliament from the Peloponnesus surmised that "If the prestige of the Greek-Americans has fallen it is only because they have lost

---

[1] For notes to chap. 6, see p. 144.

their money. Nor should one place too much stock in what the Athenians have to say about them. The Athenians think about themselves and are unconcerned about the rest...." A newspaper publisher from Tripolis agreed: "The immigrant is a greatly respected man. With few exceptions, these people are progressive in outlook and are of some consequence in Tripolis and the villages around the city. The central government of Greece does little for the rural areas. The Greek-Americans do many things for these villages." A nomarch from Crete explained: "The returned Greek-Americans are progressive, individually and socially.... They are generous to the point of being childish. They don't know how to lie, but in due time they learn if they have forgotten." A bank clerk on one of the Aegean islands said: "These people form a part of the island economy. They leave a good impression." A Rhodes labor leader added: "The Greek-Americans are boastful but kinder people."

A contrary position was taken by two persons of influence on the island of Crete. A European-educated mayor of one of the large cities dismissed the subject in a deprecating tone: "Few Greek-Americans of any account have returned to Greece. Those who have returned are people of small consequence." A newspaper publisher declared, in an obnoxious and contemptuous manner, that returned immigrants usually lived in the villages, and that his newspaper paid attention to them only when they had something to give to the community.

Members of the so-called better classes in Athens, more so than others, adopted a scornful attitude. They regarded the Greek-American in the same light as Europeans regarded the *nouveau riche*. Although repatriates hardly belonged in this category, they were still considered as ignorant brutes who had money and bad manners, but little else.

The attitude of the international set toward the Greek-American was reported as a brutal one. The American-born wife of a Greek citizen told of the mild horror expressed by a few socially prominent women when they learned of the impending marriage of the wealthy offspring of a prosperous immigrant into one of the destitute first families of the land. One or two instances of such intermarriage actually occurred, but others met with resistance.

Americans in Athens also tended to react toward repatriates in the same way as some Athenians did. Whether their reactions stemmed from their individual, independent judgment, or merely reflected the attitudes of the company they kept, was not a matter of great significance. Observed one American: "... They [the Greek-Americans] tended to irritate the Greeks of higher intellectual and cultural levels.... Culturally and spiritually these people have had little to offer Greece. They are not of the type.... I hardly believe they have been a constructive force. The ones returning are the maladjusted ones who usually try to solve problems by going away.... On the whole, they do create a bad impression." Another American, who had also spent many years in Greece, commented: "Some Greek-Americans have acquired a sort of commanding air and display it to the resentment of a good many local Greek people. Many Greek-Americans are spoken of with contempt by the fashionable Greek set. This attitude filters down into the lower ranks."

If much of the contempt for the returned immigrant was richly deserved, a fair amount of it was unjustifiable and probably stemmed from sheer jealousy and envy, and perhaps from the repatriate's tendency to flout custom and tradition. Local people, seeing evidences of the repatriates' material comfort, craved some of it for themselves, and perhaps derived satisfaction from spreading exaggerated stories of the behavior of Greek-Americans. Those who considered themselves on a higher social plane resented the apparent economic well-being of others whom they deemed socially inferior. The wife of a life-long civil servant said in a condescending manner that her landlord was a former chestnut vendor who had made his money on the streets of an American city. It irked her to have to pay rent to such a man. Others were shocked to see a substantial hotel owner, just returned from the United States, washing his own automobile instead of providing employment for one of the less fortunate. Another Greek-American was observed helping his wife hang out the family wash; this performance disgusted the proud Greek male who disapproved of anything savoring of equality between the sexes.

Various returned Greek-Americans said that their popularity rose and declined in accordance with the amount of financial aid they doled out, and that the former patronizing attitude of a relative turned into scorn once such assistance ceased.

In a broader sense the returned immigrants might be viewed as reformers who lost patience with the old established way of doing things. As a rule, reformers are too aggressive and critical to be popular. The repatriates came back with good intentions, moved by a youthful and vigorous optimism that was characteristically American. Their attitudes were like those of indiscreet Americans who traveled abroad and who expressed similar sentiments to their acquaintances. The Greek-American knew some Greek and gave vent to his feelings. Life appeared unsystematic and disorganized; the people lacked a sense of timeliness and, moreover, were hemmed in by customs and traditions that made changes difficult. A clash between Greeks and Greek-Americans was inevitable; in fact, it would have been unusual if such a conflict had not taken place.

Their unhappy experiences in Greece after 1940 caused many Greek-Americans to reassess life in the United States as contrasted to life in their native land. Whatever misgivings they might have had about the relative merits of living in America were washed away by the tragedies of the Second World War, the Nazi occupation, and the civil war of 1944–1949. Privileges and opportunities they once took for granted in the United States assumed new significance. The dominant role of Americans in the postwar period intensified their affections for a country and people they once had known. Their hearts filled with pride, and they quickly took their positions among the most Americanophile of the Americanophiles in 1947, when they saw the United States accept the invitation of the Greek government to help rehabilitate its war-torn economy.

Once tragedy struck, Greek-Americans immediately began to reminisce about the better days they had known in the United

States—how they had labored, saved, and enjoyed themselves. Such recollections were sometimes so exaggerated as to create the impression that they, the Greek-Americans, had once been integral parts of the communities in which they had lived. Some of the tales they recited were romantic in nature, almost as fanciful as the stories they had told of life in Greece when they were living in the United States. It was amusing, yet somehow pathetic, to hear a returned immigrant compare living costs in Greece in 1953 with the lower living costs he had known in America during the 1920's, as though the economy of the United States had remained stationary. One hunger-crazed repatriate recalled his dream during the war of returning to America after the fighting ceased to get his fill of the pork chops and steaks he once had known so well. The strong misgivings these people might previously have had over mixed marriages, the weakening of family ties, and the loss of the faith and tongue of their fathers, were forgotten in the tide of tragedy that engulfed them.

Many repatriates rose to oratorical heights when they spoke of the opportunities offered by the United States. It was common for them to speak of the chances they had had to work, save, deposit their money in banks, make plans for the future, and go about their daily lives without being checked by the police. One excited Greek-American told how he had entered the United States with ease and had found a job, and how he then in his stupidity thought that by returning to Greece he would be transformed into a happier man. Another shamelessly admitted that it was in the United States that he had worn his first pair of shoes, bought his first new shirt, learned to bathe regularly, and enjoyed a few of the conveniences of life. Most of them conceded that they first learned the meaning of systematic work in America. If they labored long and hard, they earned livable wages; if there was unemployment, those without jobs were few in proportion to those gainfully employed. One did not have to be a political favorite or a person of social rank to obtain an ordinary government post. Much was made of the American psychology of faith and confidence. Opportunities such as those found in the United States bred a spirit of tolerance and good will, but their absence was conducive to a spirit of intolerance and malice. The Americans possessed an optimistic spirit which the people of nations ravaged by wars, political turmoil, and economic insecurity were unable to duplicate.

Despite the general tendency of Greek-Americans to idolize the United States and remember its brighter aspects, a few of them found grounds for criticism. They recalled the complexities of life, the lawlessness, the robberies, divorces, lax morals, and the drunken men and women whom they had seen. Then, too, they had worked hard in the United States, and they could never forget it. "I didn't like it because I worked like a mule," said one. "One thing I will always remember about America," remarked another, "was that I gave it the most productive years of my life." The fast tempo, the mechanical, monotonous ways of the people, the unfair methods of competition—big business squeezing out little business, for example—were aspects of life that held little appeal for immigrant Greeks.

Some repatriates spoke with resentment about the discriminatory treatment to which they had been subjected, and expressed contempt for the supercilious airs of members of other national groups whom they considered of inferior stock and culture. Discrimination was freshest in the minds of those who went to America before the First World War. One flourishing returned Greek-American said that in 1920 he and his two brothers had been driven out of business in a rather substantial Texas community by the Ku Klux Klan, and that buyers then offered to buy them out at about five cents on the dollar.

A number of repatriates were provoked because they could not reënter the United States. Many claimed that they had come to Greece only for a visit, and that family difficulties or other personal involvements had made it impossible for them to depart within the legally prescribed time limit; they saw little justice in being barred from reëntering the United States on such grounds. One disgruntled repatriate remarked that now that the United States no longer needed cheap labor, it refused to admit those who had nothing but their labor to offer. Another, with more seriousness than humor, complained of the American preference for Anglo-Saxon peoples, and heatedly added that the Greeks were civilized when the North American continent was overrun with wild Indians and when the people of western and northern Europe were living in caves, wielding clubs, and "even practicing cannibalism."

Loss of citizenship rights angered others. "The British protect their citizens wherever they are and regardless of the number of years they have been away," complained one Greek-American. Elaborating on this point, another added: "No Greek-American in his right mind can be ungrateful or unfriendly toward the United States. He owes much to the country and he knows it. The grievance of many . . . is over the loss of citizenship rights. . . . They fail to understand this. They want freedom to come and go. They can't understand why something given them should be taken away."

Some Greek-Americans complained of their treatment at the hands of American consular officials who, they insisted, were arbitrary, self-important, and condescending. They complained of being treated like cattle, or like second-rate people. One repatriate took offense because an official advised him that if he was the good American citizen he claimed to be, he would have remained in the United States and not have come to Greece to live and die. Consular officers, on the other hand, accused repatriates of confusing falsehood with truth, especially after they had overstayed the legally prescribed time, and thus of aggravating their hardships.

There was little question about the solidly pro-American sentiments of the returned immigrants. They might have had their differences with consular officers and Americans as individuals, and perhaps have expressed their dislike for them, but never for the United States as a nation. The editor of an island newspaper observed: "These returned Greeks are forever propagandists for the United States. They talk endlessly about their stay in America." Another said, ". . . The Greeks cling to customs and traditions and can't be assimilated too easily. But the United States has done something to them.... These people have been aided by their stay in the United States and feel they are a part of the country that has given them so much...."

The outcropping of Greek-American organizations among returned immigrants reflected the favorable sentiments toward the United States. The American Legion, Department of Greece, was one of the most conspicuous. The Legion was first established in 1926–1927, and posts eventually appeared in Athens, Salonika, Patras, Chania [Crete], and Tripolis. The members were veterans of the First World War. A familiar sight in the patriotic parades of these cities, Legion leaders claimed that they had done more to promote good will between the United States and Greece than had any other group. One member triumphantly boasted that every Legionnaire was a "little Voice of America" by himself, advocating the best interests of the United States without additional expense to the American taxpayers. Americans in Greece, however, were inclined to view the organization with amusement, branding the members as pseudo patriots who, if honest in their convictions, would have returned to the United States to live. Some people viewed the American Legion in Greece as an agency designed to protect the veteran and secure his monthly pension or disability payment, and only incidentally as a group interested in the welfare of the United States.[2]

Other Greek-American organizations were the Hellenic-American Society, the American Hellenic Educational Progressive Association (AHEPA), and the Greek-American Progressive Association (GAPA). The Hellenic-American Society, once headed by a former Greek Ambassador to the United States, was chiefly a social organization with an amorphous structure; its chief functions were weekly social gatherings and sponsorship of an American study program. The AHEPA and GAPA, although founded in the United States, demonstrated an unfaltering interest in the birthplace of their members. They organized annual excursions to Greece, whose purpose, as officially stated, was to foster good will between the people of the two countries, bring much-needed American dollars to Greece, and give the members a chance to visit their homeland.'

Although there was little doubt about the dollar importance of the annual pilgrimage from the United States, serious misgivings were expressed in some quarters about the excursionists' efficacy as ambassadors of good will. Members of AHEPA and GAPA might well have been "the swallows that came to Greece every spring," especially to those delegated to greet them and to relatives who had good reasons for wanting to see them, but to many others they were nothing but "Brooklides" and *Kounesmenoi*. Their banquets were "boring, drawn out, long-winded affairs." Members, when visiting in Greece, were accused of behaving as American tourists often behaved, and of becoming carping critics when they saw things done in a manner different from that to which they had grown accustomed. They were characterized as cigar-smoking, Cadillac-driving, fez-wearing Greek-Americans who were wallowing in wealth and who behaved as Legionnaires and Elks during their respective convention weeks.

Such accounts were probably fabrications or exaggerated versions of what isolated individuals saw. Many Greek-Americans smoked cigars, a few drove Cadillacs, and a number wore fezes, which in the United States was a sign of membership in a secret society but in Greece served only as a reminder of the days of Turkish rule. The natives had never been exposed to this behavior until the Americanized Greeks arrived, and they tended to accept it as the normal but eccentric behavior of the immigrant returning from the United States.

Another type of Greek-American, whose presence left many of the local people with mixed feelings, was the aged one who returned to spend his declining years in Greece or to marry a young girl. In recent years this group has consisted of those planning to live on their social security earnings. The sight of the aged coming back to Greece to die and be buried simply confirmed the convictions of those who contended that he was the only type of person who would return. This provided fuel for the argument that the United States had more to take from Greece than to give it. These people had left Greece young and virile and they returned aged, broken in body and spirit. The receipt of social security earnings helped counteract some of these unfavorable impressions, especially when the immigrant was amply fortified with funds to aid his family and relatives.

Another distinct group consisted of the children of Greek-Americans who were born in the United States but had been taken to Greece by their parents at an early age. These children had no opportunity to know the land of their birth. They spent the most formative years of their life in Greece, and consequently were raised as Greeks. After the Second World War a number of them came to the United States as mature people to find those opportunities they had heard so much about. Frequently, the early years in America were as trying for the children as they had been for the parents, except that the younger generation often had relatives who were sufficiently established in business to give them the type of aid their parents were never able to obtain. Some adjusted themselves to the American scene readily, but others found life in the United States unsatisfactory and returned to Greece at the earliest opportunity. The latter element carried back a dreary picture of life in the United States.

After the lapse of years, some repatriates naturally had views on the subject of emigration and repatriation that were born of hindsight. Almost all of them spoke of the wisdom of emigrating to the United States, but only a minority talked about the wisdom of repatriating themselves. One repatriate complained that the natives did not consider the Greek-American a Greek and that the Americans did not consider him an American; he was a man without a country, a foreigner in his own land. Even stronger sentiments were voiced by another who viewed the whole matter with some bitterness. "One is better off by not emigrating. In the United States I worked hard and had money, but I felt insecure. I wanted to be with people who understood me, spoke the same language; I resented being called a goddam

Greek, not feeling at home, and dying in a place other than my country. On returning to Greece I discovered some resentment because I was an American. The people said, 'Go get him, he's got it [meaning money].' You come back and see poverty. That makes you think of the United States. That is why I say one is better off by not leaving the place of his birth."

CHAPTER SEVEN

SOME GREEK-AMERICAN INFLUENCES

GREEK-AMERICANS who chose to remain in the United States and those who repatriated themselves both rendered incalculable material and psychological benefits to Greece. Physical assistance, as the more obvious, was emphasized more than psychological aid which, since it was intangible in character and hence more difficult to assess, was generally ignored.

One of the most important kinds of material help given by Greek-Americans was financial. A prospective repatriate was often a steady remitter of money while he lived in the United States. His sense of altruism and the knowledge that he was soon to return made him all the more sensitive to the needs of his kin in Greece. But the expatriate as well as the repatriate helped. Besides sending money, both contributed toward village improvements and subscribed to national defense projects. The Greeks grew accustomed to expect this kind of assistance, which was spread out over a long period of time, from their American relatives. Gradually a tradition of Greek-American aid was built up. Later this was implemented and expanded, though in a different form, by the Greek War Relief Association, UNNRA, the American Mission to Aid Greece, and finally by the Mutual Security Administration.[1]

Money remittances were the first substantial contributions, and were sent from the United States to support parents, help discharge family debts, maintain, improve, or purchase addi-

---

[1] For notes to chap. 7, see pp. 144–146.

tional property, deposit in banks, or lend out for a return. An idea of how significant these remittances were can be gained from the statement that "... remittances from America through the National Bank alone amounted to 27 per cent of the public receipts and 20 per cent of the public expenditures in the year 1919; and to 57 per cent of the public receipts and 38 per cent of the public expenditures in the year 1920." Many Greeks dreaded to think what their villages would be like without Greek-American aid. "Good times in Tarpon Springs, Florida, meant good times on my home island," reported one. An American who investigated the economic status of the repatriated on the island of Karpathos in the Dodecanese estimated that in 1952 "there [were] about 5,000 Karpathians living in the United States, and bank sources report[ed] that monthly aid checks from these relatives amounted to between twenty and thirty thousand dollars in addition to gifts of clothing and food."[2]

The importance of these remittances was first suggested by the volume of registered mail—a common way of sending money from the United States—received in Greece. Only 52,068 pieces of such mail passed through the Athens post office in 1901, but 162,895 pieces passed through in 1905. Meanwhile, the number of postal money orders had risen from 409 in 1902 to 10,007 in 1905, and their value had increased from $13,295 to $346,993. The total value of postal money orders was $650,203 in 1906, some $2,099,843 in 1907, and about $5,000,000 in 1908. In 1909 the total dropped to $2,219,297.[3]

These remittances and the wholesale transference of life savings from the United States pumped money into the economic life of the villages. A Greek commission noted very early the effect of this financial assistance on the homeland. In 1906 it concluded that "No one can deny that it is to them in great measure ... that we owe the rise in the value of our paper currency almost to par.... Everyone mentions ... that in these provinces, particularly in Peloponnesus, which are the oldest and most prolific sources of emigration to the United States, there has been a striking fall in the rate of interest and a proportionate rise in the value of agricultural real estate...."[4]

GREEK-AMERICAN INFLUENCES

A member of the Greek Parliament described the effects of Greek-American aid in more precise terms: "In Epidaurus-Limira ... influences of emigration have become conspicuous and tangible in many respects. Villages have grown into towns. There has been an increased number of churches built.... Property has gone up considerably in value and is being cultivated more systematically, and, chief of all, usury is receding, fleeing from the glitter of abundant gold which has inundated towns and villages. In some of these villages checks for hundreds of francs remain uncashed owing to the fall in exchange during the past year. Nor is it surprising that the rate of interest should have fallen from 20, 15, and 10 per cent to 6 and 5 per cent. And in other villages where not long ago the appearance of a creditor used to strike terror to the hearts of debtors, today the arrival of a would-be debtor in search of a loan invokes the interest of the moneyed villagers, each of whom seeks the privilege of making a loan."[5]

These remittances increased steadily until they reached the unprecedented levels of the post-World War I era. From approximately $4,675,000 in 1910 they rose to more than $72,000,000 in 1919 and to $110,000,000 in 1920. From then on the amounts declined and never again reached the levels of 1919–1921 (see table 6).[6]

There were several reasons for the decline after 1921. The immigrants who repatriated themselves naturally ceased being the abundant source of financial assistance they had been while they were in America, and the immigration bars raised by the United States kept out others who might have become steady remitters. Similarly, the long residence of many of the older immigrants in America weakened their ties with the homeland and lessened their desire to send money. The forced loan floated by the Greek government heightened suspicion among Greek-Americans. The ensuing political and economic instability of the 1920's and the early 1930's, combined with the growing desire of Greek immigrants in the United States to retreat from the Old World, emotionally and otherwise, reflected itself in the diminishing remittances. Also, more Greek immigrants were becoming citizens of the United States. Many who previously had been in the habit of forwarding money to Greece for deposit in banks or for investment purposes began to invest instead in American real estate and business enterprises. In effect these multiple developments dried up thousands of small sources of financial assistance, and made the decline in remittances inevitable.[7]

TABLE 6

IMMIGRANT REMITTANCES RECEIVED IN GREECE, 1910–1950
(In thousands of dollars)

Year	Amount	Year	Amount
1910	$ 4,675	1931	$32,387
1911	3,365	1932	7,352
1912	5,688	1933	18,600
1913	5,498	1934	14,700
1914	8,228	1935	10,300
1915	10,216	1936	16,600
1916	10,923	1937	30,400
1917	12,560	1938	24,700
1918	24,644	1939	15,400
1919	72,285	1940[a]	......
1920	110,077	1941[a]	......
1921	73,371	1942[a]	......
1922	23,901	1943[a]	......
1923	32,976	1944[a]	......
1924	42,246	1945	24,500
1925	36,399	1946	37,900
1926	37,120	1947	15,900
1927	37,997	1948	11,100
1928	31,293	1949	8,600
1929	38,059	1950	14,300
1930	40,666		

[a] No remittances were sent during the Second World War.
SOURCES: See note 6 to chap. 7, p. 145.

Beginning in 1940, however, the interest of Greek expatriates in their homeland revived. The heroic role of Greece in checking the legions of Mussolini made many a once reluctant Greek-American praise his compatriots with renewed vigor. This moral support was combined with financial, technical, and material aid after 1944–1945. Money, clothing, medicine, food, farm ani-

GREEK-AMERICAN INFLUENCES

mals, and various other supplies were rushed to the stricken land. Thousands of Greeks were fed, clothed, and otherwise provided for by the generous contributions of American relatives. This aid was beyond and above that forwarded by the United States government. A field representative of the Mutual Security Administration in Greece asserted that Greek-Americans in the United States frequently wrote to his office inquiring about the needs of a particular village, and seeking information as to what they as individuals, or the MSA as an agency, could do for the village.[8]

Emigration and repatriation also affected commercial and trade relations between the United States and Greece. For instance, they were responsible for the establishment of direct steamship service between the two countries. Previous efforts had ended in failure, but when the service was established, it was recognized as due to "the emigrant movement, back to and from the United States."

The "back-and-forth" movement of the immigrants also created markets for the products of both countries. The repatriate took back with him newly acquired tastes and helped create a demand for American products in Greece. Although small at first, these markets were destined to grow with the passage of time. The demand for American goods soon spread among the Greek population. In 1908 the American Consul in Athens observed that "A family that came to Greece to live for a term of years imported an American range, and several Greeks who saw it were so pleased with it that they ordered similar ones." In reverse fashion, emigrants arriving in the United States for the first time carried their old-world tastes with them. Consequently, they created an American market for Greek cheese, black olives, and other native products. In short, the immigrant became a genuine "commercial emissary."[9]

Prominent Greek banking firms likewise capitalized on the strong attachment of the immigrants to their birthplace. As early as 1908, a Greek-American bank was established in Athens to cater to the mounting immigrant traffic. In 1919 the National Bank of Greece sent a mission to the United States to explore the

GREEK-AMERICAN INFLUENCES

possibilities of establishing a branch there. These efforts continued until 1929 when the Hellenic Bank Trust Company was formed in New York City.[10]

Perhaps better publicized were the activities of the Bank of Athens which opened a branch in New York City and published a monthly periodical, entitled *News from Greece,* to serve a Greek-American clientele.[11] The publication advertised investment opportunities in Greece and sought to facilitate the efforts of those Greek-Americans whose concern for relatives in the homeland had never ceased. *News from Greece* circulated during the years between 1926 and 1934, when much of the earlier enthusiasm for Greece in America was vanishing. The journal's first editorial said in part: "... The person living abroad, who labors in some distant land, will never have the incentive and interest in his work, unless he thinks of his elderly mother, father, the boys and his sisters, his home and distant village, his country, ... who await his financial assistance today and his happy return tomorrow, so he could lead a happy and proud life...."[12] Had this periodical appeared earlier—when interest in the homeland was very keen—it might have had greater appeal, but it came a little late. The depression of the early 1930's, and the immigrants' lack of faith in Greek financial policies, hindered the very investment opportunities that *News from Greece* tried to promote.

Equally alert were the tourist agencies, which had their eyes fixed on American dollars, and those patriotic individuals who were determined to have their American brothers remain attached to Greece. For years Greeks had expressed the fear that long residence in the United States would weaken ties with the mother country. Any program promising to regenerate and strengthen devotion to Greece among immigrants was therefore regarded with favor. As a result, travel brochures were prepared, annual pilgrimages were arranged, and newspaper stories and periodical accounts were written in order to create nostalgic memories of the homeland and to gain the sympathies of the first generation born in the United States. In fact, attempts to preserve a particularistic spirit among Greek-Americans and their offspring appear to have had the moral but unofficial support of important Greeks in and out of high office.[13]

Far more difficult to appraise was the psychological influence of returned immigrants on the mother country. Such evaluations are elusive by their very nature, and are not made any easier by the sharp differences of opinion based on personal bias.

One important influence was the spirit of progress that animated returning Greek-Americans. It was evidenced by the innovations attempted by the repatriate, the construction of new homes, the purchases of land, and the provisions he made for his family. This spirit was contagious and soon affected many villages, though spending itself more quickly in some than in others. It affected even those who had never been to the United States, breeding in them a spirit of discontent. At certain stages, especially when the repatriate first arrived in Greece, his advice might have been sought in the village. Because he had seen the latest in technological progress, construction, sanitation, hospitalization, and various other public improvements, he was frequently looked up to as a person with ideas as well as financial means. Often this flattering attitude was manufactured in order to elicit financial aid for a village project. A prominent Greek-American who periodically visited Greece observed, however, that "They [the Greek-Americans] introduced health protection measures and more sanitary ways of handling foods. They helped to standardize prices—that is, to make the marked price the selling price instead of the bazaar method of bargaining. Greek-Americans are credited with establishing cow herds, the pasteurization process, and with serving as good will ambassadors...."

As a result of his stay in the United States, the repatriate might for the first time have sensed the relationship between better roads and community progress. Since many villages were without the most elementary kinds of transportation, it is hardly surprising that the returning Greek-American, inspired by his American experiences, was in the vanguard of efforts to inaugurate improvements. Societies sponsoring such projects had his moral and financial support; funds were solicited from former villagers who resided in the larger towns and cities of Greece, but especially from those in the United States who normally were expected to carry the brunt of the financial burden. As usual, the latter responded enthusiastically to such appeals by staging money-raising campaigns, dances, benefit programs, and other affairs, and forwarding the receipts to a designated person who often turned out to be an Athenian lawyer.[14]

Unfortunately, money raised for such worthy purposes was occasionally handled inefficiently; and if some of the more pessimistic accounts are to be believed, the bulk of it was mismanaged. Poor planning, unrealistic procedures, dishonesty, and rank individualism on the part of the persons and organizations involved made for a waste of funds and energies. A Greek-American contributed an X-ray machine to a village which had neither electricity nor a person capable of operating the machine; another who gave a microscope saw his efforts wasted for similar reasons; and in still another instance many Greek-Americans helped to finance the construction of a hospital which had far more beds than the area needed. When the hospital building was completed, the authorities faced difficulties in recruiting personnel and finances required for its operation. Health centers built with Greek-American dollars were poorly located, and so could not be used efficiently. Large ambulances purchased to service these centers were expensive to maintain and clumsy to handle on the donkey paths that served as roads in rural areas. Greek-American benefactors who had grown accustomed to riding in Cadillacs or Buicks in the United States were hardly the best judges of the transportation needs of the "jackass economy" they had left years before.

Local Greeks, despite their frequent criticisms of the repatriated immigrant, spoke of the practical spirit he brought with him. The Greek-American stressed the common everyday aspects of life in the United States which he wished to transplant to Greece. Besides emphasizing the utilitarian as against the impractical and sentimental, he reflected a greater sense of timeliness, industry, and orderliness.

Because of their occupational backgrounds, repatriates might have been expected to exert some influence on the eating habits of the home folks. But this was true only in a very limited sense, because the Greek was almost as patriotic to his stomach as he was to his country. Obviously, the inevitable coffee and doughnuts were introduced into Greece, and ice-cream dishes, milk shakes, and other American fountain drinks were popularized. In several pioneer Greek-American shops, foods normally listed on American menus were spelled out in English and Greek. In these and in other places operated by Greek-Americans, an American atmosphere prevailed. For unexplained reasons Greeks never succumbed to the hamburger as Americans had, perhaps because of their preference for their own kind of food or because no single shop systematically concerned itself with the preparation of this particular American stand-by. Similarly, the "hot dog," which had done much to line the pockets of early immigrants and had thereby contributed to the maintenance of many villagers, was shamefully neglected. Only periodically could one see a vendor hawking his wares on the streets of Athens. Coca-Cola also was ignored, and rumor had it that the Greeks were never overly fond of "gassy drinks"; those that were preferred their own kind.[15]

In education, the influence of Greek-Americans was evidenced by the help they gave the young. The son of a repatriated immigrant stated: "I graduated from the University of Athens with the American-earned dollars of my father. He lived in Chicago for many years. He returned during the early 1920's. Many sons of Peloponnesians were educated with money earned in the United States...." A Greek-American who returned in 1912 said that his earnings enabled him to send his son to the university to study law. Many other young Greeks born of repatriated Greek-American parents were trained as doctors and lawyers with money earned in the United States.

The education of youth was influenced in still another respect. Sons and, to a lesser extent, daughters of some repatriates were inspired to go to the United States for undergraduate as well as graduate training. One repatriate said: "I have a daughter attending Centre College in Danville, Kentucky. She probably was influenced to go to the United States because I have been to America." A butcher-shop owner in Athens proudly asserted, "My son is attending the University of Wisconsin. He is studying engineering." A wealthy Athenian said, "I have a daughter attending Northwestern University." A former Montgomery, Alabama, restaurant keeper, now a villager in Greece, provided for his son to come to the United States for advanced medical training. Another, once a resident of St. Louis, added: "I have a daughter attending Washington University in St. Louis."

Some of these young people developed an attachment for the American way of life that made readjustment difficult when they returned to Greece. Others who did not care to go back to their native land sometimes succeeded in marrying American girls, which they hoped would insure their remaining in the United States. This preference for America was depriving Greece of skilled and professional people it could ill afford to lose, while demonstrating the pull that America continued to have for the young people of the nation.

The repatriates had little influence on trade-unionism in Greece because few trade-unionists returned there to work for a living. As a rule, the Greek-American went back to his native land to retire and "live off his investments." Those workers who did return to live in Greece were usually unskilled instead of skilled, and as such had no influence. Since many of the repatriated had formerly been small shopkeepers, they presumably had a strong antilabor bias. If there was anything constructive that a repatriated trade-unionist could have offered, it would probably have been advice as to how a particular issue had been faced by an American labor organization.[16]

From the beginning it was apparent that Greek-Americans could play a significant role in an ideological campaign in behalf of the democratic way of life. As early as 1908, the editor and publisher of *Atlantis* observed that the immigrant could easily become an instrumental force in the social and cultural elevation of his compatriots in both Greece and the unredeemed parts. In fact, this Greek-American daily conducted a short-lived campaign with that objective in mind. Circulation of the paper among nationals in Greece and Turkey would help to transplant American ideas to both countries, show them how people lived and flourished in the United States, and also provide them with a few of the educational opportunities enjoyed by their more fortunate compatriots. The circulation-minded, but equally optimistic, publisher hoped that *Atlantis* would serve as a source of inspiration for those who had only slight knowledge of the cultural opportunities and happiness to which man was entitled; that it would "transfuse American ideas" into these unfortunate areas, and "show to our [Greek] statesmen how this happy land is governed." The newspaper went on to say: "When the sound principles of Washington, Lincoln, Roosevelt and Taft bear fruit, our country [Greece], whose men first benefited, will be happier, wealthier, blissful. The holy and sacred soil of Greece and of the enslaved provinces is fertile, ready to be cultivated with the new fruit bearing seed."[17]

Many of the repatriated immigrants proved their worthiness as emissaries of the American way of life. As a provincial labor leader observed: "They bring back a more democratic spirit.... Often a returned Greek is placed on a committee to help explain how things are done in the United States. These people are freer in expressing themselves. I know of a Greek-American who served as mayor of his village for twenty-five years. I know another who served for three years.... They have a better insight into mechanical problems. They know more about machines. Many, if not most, know a little American music. They often encourage sports.... The returned Greek-Americans are staunch defenders of America. They resent and fight anti-Americanism." This same observer claimed that although many kinds of people returned from the United States, he failed to encounter a single Communist in the lot. Most repatriated immigrants were progressive in outlook, innovators, gradualists, and confirmed believers in the principle of majority rule.

Partly because of this attitude, many repatriates were eager to oppose Fascists and Nazis. During the German and Italian occupation of Greece, small bands of Greek-Americans gave their native country a unique kind of assistance. According to a British source, about 250 of them, operating in twelve groups, were dropped by parachute to harass the Nazi invaders in retreat from Greece. Most of these men had left Greece as young men and had lived in towns and cities scattered all over the United States. "Their task had been to stiffen the Andartes [the guerrillas], working in detachments of 24 men, with two officers, against exit railways such as those from Janina-Agrinion, Lamia-Salonica, Lamia-Larissa and the main Athens-Salonica railway. So successfully did they operate that the Germans dared not move their trains faster than ten or twelve miles an hour, despite the fact that they had created pill-boxes every three kilometers and guarded the line with wire and mines and troops armed with mortars and twenty-millimeter cannons. The practise of the American-Greek was to fire bazooka shells into the locomotives, tearing the tubes, and a second shell into armoured cars, before spraying the carriages with machine-gun fire. The Germans were terrified by these attacks."[18]

Various observers commented on the role of repatriated Greek-Americans during the occupation. A veteran of the First World War stated: "The Greek-Americans in Salonika aided the English . . . to escape, found them jobs, and fed them. The Nazis called me Roosevelt because I served in the United States army." A member of the American Legion in Salonika was wounded and imprisoned by the Nazis for six months. An islander, formerly a resident of Albany, New York, was arrested with many others on charges of spying for the Allies. On the island of Rhodes, in the attractive village of Kremasti, an athletic association initiated by Greek-Americans symbolized resistance.

Since repatriated Greeks came from various countries, comparisons were often made between Greek-Americans and refugees from Turkey in Europe and Asia Minor. Unfair in certain respects and meaningless in others, such comparisons did, however, bring into sharper focus the relative ease with which a person of semioriental background could adjust himself to the Greek environment.

GREEK-AMERICAN INFLUENCES

As a rule, Greek-Americans returned to Greece on their own volition in order to retire, and they arrived in relatively small numbers. Refugees, on the other hand, numbering about a million and a half, came involuntarily after the Greeks were defeated in Asia Minor in 1922. They had been happy while they lived there, and would probably have preferred to remain, but events beyond their control forced them to begin life anew. Greek-Americans came with their life's savings and a more western outlook; refugees from the Levant came penniless, often devoid of friends and relatives, and in the face of the resentment and hostility of Greek peasants. The former might have come with their money and with quickness and an alertness that were foreign to the villager, but they also came with a gullibility and a faith in the individual which, to a good many Greeks, seemed to be evidences of stupidity. They ran a poor second to the shrewd, commercial-minded, and cosmopolitan refugees from Asia Minor. The latter's adaptation to Greek ways was instantaneous, and their success in the business and industrial world unbelievably swift; they made great contributions to the Greek nation.[19]

Observers pointed out, however, that Greek-Americans and Asia Minor refugees differed sharply in their susceptibility to leftist dogmas. The latter's proximity to Russia might well have been a factor in their greater receptivity to Communist doctrines. Macedonia, portions of Thrace, the Dodecanese Islands, and refugee communities in general, which had known better days under the rule of some other power, were often singled out as the most discontented areas in Greece. In contrast with other regions, they were accused of having more than the usual number of voters supporting the extreme liberal or leftist ticket. As a result, many conservative and patriotic Greeks have within recent years developed a strong resentment against further irredentist and expansionist programs. Recently one such patriot voiced strong opposition to the incorporation of Cyprus into Greece because, he said, the inhabitants would probably recall the better times they had known under the English, and would be unhappy "if they came home to mother and had to eat onions with the rest of the Greeks."[20]

Greek-Americans were also compared with Egyptian-Greeks who came to Greece for permanent residence or for periodic vacations. Comprising a very influential element in Alexandria, and to a much lesser extent in Cairo, Egyptian-Greeks were likely to have been substantial merchants, druggists, exporters, shippers, or professional people. The typical Egyptian-Greek was a wealthier and a more cultured person than the Greek-American; he often maintained a residence on the Greek mainland or on an island, had business ties, and traveled regularly between Greece and Egypt. Like the Asia Minor refugee, the Egyptian-Greek found it easier to acclimate himself to the Greek scene than did the Greek-American.[21]

Regardless of the contributions and influences of the repatriates from different countries, there were always those who claimed that Greece lost more from emigration than it gained. Perhaps this theory was true, but it was at the same time inconsistent with former pronouncements and with the efforts of the Greek government after the Second World War to encourage emigration to foreign lands. The pressure to emigrate to the United States always was great. Those who left for America at a much earlier time found jobs and business opportunities they could probably never have equaled in Greece. If they worked long enough in the United States they earned retirement pensions and thus, after repatriation, enjoyed a higher standard of living than would have been their lot had they never left home.[22]

The repatriates who returned from the United States could not help but bring to Greece some of both the material and the intangible qualities of American life. In going from an advanced to a retarded social economy, they took with them money, higher standards of living, a spirit of optimism, reformist attitudes, and pronounced pro-American sentiments. They had come into contact with a different language, with different customs and attitudes. They could hardly have failed to acquire new skills and techniques; their tempo of life had quickened;

they had seen people worship in different churches; for better or for worse, they were exposed to the American press, periodicals, and literature; they had seen women treated differently; and they had sensed the pulsating effects of living in a strong and wealthy country. What they brought back often filtered down into the proverty-stricken areas of the country, and many of the services they and the expatriated rendered were of a character normally furnished by local governments in America. Even though their names failed to appear on the façades of the libraries, museums, and schools of Athens, their contributions were nevertheless genuine. Their devotion to Greece was more altruistic than that of their voluble critics or of the Athenians who flocked to the sidewalk cafes.[23]

APPENDIX

QUESTIONNAIRE USED IN INTERVIEWING
REPATRIATES IN GREECE

1. Name   Birthday
2. Place of birth
3. Residence in the United States
4. Length of stay in the United States
5. Occupation in the United States
6. Date of last return to Greece
7. Reasons for returning to Greece
8. If married did your family, including children, return to Greece?
9. How did the members of your family feel about returning?
10. Did you return to your native village? If not, where did you go?
11. If you returned to the village, how did you like life there in comparison with the one you knew in the United States?
12. Were you an American citizen at the time of your return? Are you still an American citizen? If your citizenship rights were lost, what accounted for this?
13. How did your friends and relatives react to your return from the United States?
14. Did you think you did the right thing in returning to Greece at the time you did?
15. What advantages does living in Greece offer you as against living in the United States?
16. What appealed to you the most in the United States? Why?
17. What appealed to you the least? Why?
18. Economically, are you as well off now as you were then?
19. Are you happier living in Greece? If the answer is yes, explain why.

APPENDIX

20. Would you return to the United States to live permanently if the opportunity was made available again?
21. Has your stay in the United States made you a happier man?
22. What in your opinion was the greatest contribution that the United States has made to your life?
23. In your opinion what permanent good have the Greek-Americans brought to Greece? What evidence is there of this?
24. In your opinion have the Greek-Americans created ill-will in Greece? Why? What evidence is there of this?

NOTES

CHAPTER ONE

AMERICA AND THE GREEK IMMIGRANT

[1] Peter Roberts, *The New Immigration* (New York, 1920), p. vii.
[2] Emmanuel S. Lekoude, *The Immigrants* (*E Metanastai*) (Athens, 1903), pp. 12–13; G. M. Marinou, *The Nation of Wealth* (*To Kratos Tou Ploutou*) (Athens, 1904), *passim;* N. Gkortzi, *America and Americans* (*Ameriki Kai Amerikani*) (Athens, 1907?), *passim;* Konstantinos D. Maniakes, *America and Greece* (Athens, 1899), *passim; Reports of the Immigration Commission,* Vol. IV, *Emigration Conditions in Europe,* U.S. 61st Cong., 3d sess., S. Doc. 748 (Washington, 1911), p. 394 (hereafter cited as *Emigration Conditions in Europe*); Emmanuel Repouli, *A Study on Immigration with Suggested Legislation* (*Meleti Meta Schediou Nomou Peri Metanasteuseos*) (Athens, 1912), pp. 20–23; *Atlantis,* Mar. 31, 1909.
[3] Harold U. Faulkner, *The Decline of Laissez Faire, 1897–1917* (New York, 1951), pp. 6–10; William Miller, *A History of the Greek People, 1821–1921* (London, 1922), pp. 99–110; *Economic Journal,* V (June, 1895), 285–288; IX (Dec., 1899), 634–651; XVI (Dec., 1906), 597–601.
[4] Lekoude, *op. cit.,* p. 4; Repouli, *op. cit.,* pp. 34–58; Henry P. Fairchild, *Greek Immigration to the United States* (New Haven, 1911), pp. 58–82.
[5] Lekoude, *op. cit.,* p. 29.
[6] *Ibid.,* p. 35.
[7] Repouli, *op. cit.,* p. 34.
[8] Fairchild, *op. cit.,* pp. 83–105; Repouli, *op. cit.,* p. 56.
[9] Lekoude, *op. cit.,* p. 32.
[10] *Ibid.,* p. 4.
[11] *E Sphaira,* Apr. 5, 1907; *Greek Immigration, with an Introduction by Andreas M. Andreadou* (*Helleniki Metanasteusis, Meta Prologou Andreas M. Andreadou*) (Athens, 1917), pp. 76, 251–252 (hereafter cited as Andreades, *Helleniki Metanasteusis*).
[12] Lekoude, *op. cit.,* pp. 5–6.
[13] The dowry system is mentioned briefly, but accurately, in Rennell Rodd, *The Custom and Lore of Modern Greece* (London, 1892), p. 92, and is touched upon in Lucy M. J. Garnett, *Greece of the Hellenes* (New York, 1914), p. 214. For emigration of females see Garnett, *op. cit.,* p. 133, and *Emigration Conditions in Europe,* p. 392. Available figures show that, of the 186,016 Greeks in the United States by 1911, some 170,775 or 94.5 per cent were males, and 9,883 or 5.5 per cent were females. According to the Toledo *News-Bee,* only 125 of the estimated 3,000 Greeks living in the city in 1922 were women. See also *National Herald* (*Ethnikos Kyrix*), Dec. 10, 1922, p. 8; Michael Choukas, "Greek-Americans," in *Our Racial and National Minorities,* ed. by F. J. Brown and J. S. Roucek (New York, 1937), p. 342.
[14] Perhaps the most vocal of the contemporary periodicals was *Hellenismos,* published by the society for the promotion of Hellenism. See also

NOTES

Aristedes E. Phoutrides, "The Literary Impulses of Modern Greece," *Poet Lore*, XXVI (Jan.-Feb., 1915), 56.

[15] *To Kratos*, Aug. 26, 1912; *Atlantis*, Mar. 24, 1909; Andreades, *Helleniki Metanasteusis*, pp. 322-324, 342-344; Repouli, *op. cit.*, pp. 82-83; Alexis Krikou, *The Status of Hellenism in America (E Theshis Tou Hellenismou En Ameriki)* (Athens, 1915), p. 212.

[16] *E Sphaira*, Nov. 20, 1907; *Atlantis*, Jan. 14, 1909; Repouli, *op. cit.*, p. 11.

[17] Repouli, *op. cit.*, pp. 15, 17-18; Elias I. Janetis, *His Eminence, the Immigrant (E Autou Megaliotis, O Metanastis)* (New York, 1946), pp. 9-10, 27-34.

[18] Baumbi Malafouris, *Greeks in America, 1528-1948* (New York, 1948), pp. 109-110, 112, 123.

[19] *Emigration Conditions in Europe*, p. 394.

[20] This "grab-and-run" behavior of the immigrant has not been as fully studied as it should be. American writers usually speak of such an immigrant as the "bird of passage," whereas the Greeks spoke of his coming to "grab and run."

[21] See N. Gkortzi, *Ameriki Kai Amerikani*, pp. 69-72, for criticism of the Greek immigrant for his failure to become a farmer. See also *California*, Oct. 20, Nov. 24, 1917; Nov. 9, 1918; Oct. 25, 1919.

[22] *To Kratos*, Nov. 8, 1907; *E Sphaira*, Nov. 10, 1907; *Illustrated Monthly Atlantis*, III (Apr., 1912), 15-17; Malafouris, *op. cit.*, pp. 117-138.

[23] E. E. Weyl, "Pericles of Smyrna and New York," *The Outlook*, XCIV (Feb. 26, 1910), 472.

[24] Michael A. Dendia, *Greek Colonies around the World (Hellenikai Parikiae Ana Ton Kosmon)* (Athens, 1919), pp. 87-88; Malafouris, *op. cit.*, p. 116; Janetis, *op. cit.*, p. 107.

[25] Repouli, *op. cit.*, pp. 154-155.

[26] Malafouris, *op. cit.*, p. 110.

[27] *Ibid.*, pp. 117-127; Dendia, *op. cit.*, p. 90.

[28] Janetis, *op. cit.*, p. 27.

[29] Numerous repatriated immigrants referred to the long exhausting hours of work.

[30] Malafouris, *op. cit.*, p. 276.

[31] Janetis, *op. cit.*, pp. 21-22, 27; *Report of the Commission on the Problem of Immigration in Massachusetts* (Boston, 1914), pp. 66-67.

[32] Kyotchek S. Christowe, *Outlook*, CLV (May 14, 1930), 48-49. See *Atlantis*, Feb. 23-27, Mar. 1, 1909, for an account of the worst anti-Greek riot in the United States. See also *ibid.*, Jan. 18, 1908.

[33] The most pointed comments were made by the immigrants themselves.

[34] *Emigration from Greece, a Report of the Committee of Parliament (E Ex Hellados Metanasteusis, E Ekthesis Tis Epitropis Tis Voulis)* (Athens, 1906), pp. 10-11; Repouli, *op. cit.*, pp. 98-103; John W. Brown, *World Migration and Labor* (Amsterdam, 1926), pp. 14-15.

[35] See Fairchild, *op. cit.*, pp. 120-164, for accounts of some of the early Greek colonies in the United States.

[36] Malafouris, *op. cit.*, pp. 175-187; Krikou, *op. cit.*, pp. 81-92; chapter entitled "Religion and the Church," K. K. Joacheim, *The Dangers Facing Hellenism in America and the Means for Its Salvation (E Kindinoi Tou En Ameriki Hellinismou Kai Ta Mesa Tis Diasoseos Autou)* (Boston, 1926), pp. 12-17; *To Kratos*, July 12, 1907; *Atlantis*, July 21, Dec. 26, 1908; Apr. 17, 1909; Apr. 26, 1922. Regarding the formation of the Greek Re-

NOTES

formed Church in the United States, see *To Kratos*, Dec. 17, 1909; June 10, Oct. 28, 1910.

[37] Christowe, *Outlook*, CLV (May 14, 1930), 48–49; *Atlantis*, Jan. 3, 1913; Malafouris, *op. cit.*, p. 115.

[38] J. P. Xenides, *The Greeks in America* (New York, 1922), p. 88.

[39] *Atlantis*, Nov. 17, 1908; Jan. 21, 1909; Jan. 3, 1913.

[40] Xenides, *op. cit.*, p. 88.

[41] Peter Roberts, *op. cit.*, pp. 272–273; Paul McPharlin, *The Puppet Theatre in America, a History, 1524 to Now* (New York, 1949), pp. 289–291. Relevant information came also from an interview with an early *karagiozi* performer in the United States who currently resides in a small village outside Tripolis, Greece.

[42] *Atlantis*, July 3, 1912; M. M. Davis, *Immigrant Health and the Community* (New York, 1921), pp. 101–102; Malafouris, *op. cit.*, pp. 191–226.

[43] Virtually nothing has appeared on this phase of immigrant life. Although the Greek professional athletes were scarce by comparison with those of other nationality groups, the few who managed to gain the spotlight had a spirited following among their compatriots.

[44] See, for instance, D. Callimachos, "Lessons for the Greeks of America," ("Epodeigmata Pros Tous Hellines Tis Amerikis") in the *Tenth Anniversary Edition of the National Herald (Dekaetris Ethnikou Kyrikos)*, XI (Apr., 1925), 65–66; Andreades, *Helleniki Metanasteusis*, pp. 49–50.

[45] Malafouris, *op. cit.*, pp. 227–247.

[46] *Ibid.*, pp. 228–229; *Panhellenios*, Oct. 16, 1908; *Illustrated Monthly Atlantis (Menea Ekonographimeni Atlantis)*, I (Dec., 1910), 26–28; *Report of the Commission on the Problem of Immigration in Massachusetts*, pp. 201–202.

CHAPTER TWO

MOTIVES, ATTITUDES, AND STATUS OF THE REPATRIATED GREEK

[1] Aristotelis Kourtides, "Immigration and the School," *Study (E Meleti)*, I, No. 5 (May, 1907), 258–262.

[2] *New York Evening Sun*, as quoted in *Atlantis*, May 2, 1908; *E Sphaira*, Feb. 10, May 2, 1907; *Panhellenios Kratos*, June 26, 1908; *To Kratos*, Nov. 26, 1909; *Emigration from Greece, a Report of the Committee of Parliament* (Athens, 1906), pp. 10–11; Emmanuel Repouli, *A Study on Immigration with Suggested Legislation* (Athens, 1912), pp. 98–103.

[3] Emmanuel S. Lekoude, *The Immigrants* (Athens, 1903), pp. 64–66; *E Sphaira*, Feb. 19, Apr. 5, 1907; *To Kratos*, July 15, 1907; Alexis Krikou, *The Status of Hellenism in America* (Athens, 1915), p. 212.

[4] *E Sphaira*, Nov. 17, 22, Dec. 5, 1907.

[5] *Panhellenios*, Aug. 6, 1908.

[6] *To Kratos*, Nov. 25, 1907; *Panhellenios Kratos*, Apr. 19, 1908.

[7] *Atlantis*, Feb. 4, 5, 6, 1909.

[8] *Ibid.*, Feb. 15, 1896; Mar. 12, 26, Apr. 23, Oct. 29, 1897.

[9] Baumbi Malafouris, *Greeks in America, 1528–1948* (New York, 1948), pp. 194–196.

[10] *Great Hellenic Encyclopaedia (Megale Helleniki Enkeklopaedia)* (Athens, 1930), XVI, 778; *E Sphaira*, Jan. 9, 1907; *Atlantis*, Jan. 15, 1908.

[11] *Atlantis*, Aug. 13, 1909; Jan. 30, 1913; *Panhellenios Kratos*, Aug. 29, 1909; *To Kratos*, July 18, Aug. 21, 1910.

NOTES

¹² *To Kratos*, Sept. 16, Dec. 16, 1912.
¹³ *Ibid.*, Jan. 20, May 26, Sept. 1, 1913.
¹⁴ Michael Choukas, "Greek-Americans," in F. J. Brown and J. S. Roucek, eds., *Our Racial and National Minorities* (New York, 1937), p. 340; *National Herald*, Dec. 10, 1922; *New York Times*, July 3, 1923.
¹⁵ This spirit is expressed in an article appearing in the newspaper *Vima* (Athens), May 16, 1950.
¹⁶ For a Greek definition of a Greek, see Panteli E. Kerkinou, *Greek Citizenship in Egypt (E Helleniki Ithayenia En Agypto)* (Alexandria, Egypt, 1930), pp. 12–14. See also a pamphlet entitled *Information for Bearers of Passports*, U.S. Department of State, Feb. 1, 1952, pp. 71–76; Malafouris, *op. cit.*, p. 108; *Abstract of Reports of the Immigration Commission* (Washington, 1911), I, 243–45.
¹⁷ *Reports of the Immigration Commission, Statistical Review of Immigration, 1820–1910*, U.S. 61st Cong., 3d. sess., S. Doc. 756 (Washington, 1911), pp. 372, 383–384; Repouli, *op. cit.*, pp. 12–13.
¹⁸ Figures for 1908 to 1921 were taken from the *Annual Report of the Commissioner General of Immigration, Fiscal Year Ended June 30, 1921*, U.S. Department of Labor (Washington, 1921), pp. 108–111; for 1921 to 1931, *Annual Report of the Commissioner General of Immigration, Fiscal Year Ended June 30, 1931* (Washington, 1931), pp. 224–228; *Annual Report of the Commissioner General of Immigration, Fiscal Year Ended June 30, 1932* (Washington, 1932), pp. 74–75; National Bureau of Economic Research, *International Migrations* (New York, 1929), I, 93. Figures for 1933 to 1952 were compiled from the *Statistical Abstract of the United States*.
¹⁹ *Annual Report of the Commissioner of Immigration, Fiscal Year Ended June 30, 1920*, U.S. Department of Labor (Washington, 1920), pp. 98, 104.
²⁰ For the figures cited, the author had to rely rather heavily on the revelations of the returned immigrants themselves. Some were very willing to reveal the exact amount they brought back; others were hesitant, or simply refused. Occasionally the reluctance to reveal any large sum stemmed from fear of yielding information that would be the basis for prosecution.
²¹ Malafouris, *op. cit.*, pp. 263–264; Repouli, *op. cit.*, pp. 102–103.
²² *O Xeniteumenos*, Jan. 17, 31, 1935.

CHAPTER THREE

READJUSTMENT IN GREEK SOCIETY

¹ *O Xeniteumenos*, Jan. 17, 1935; E. P. X., "The Dream of the Immigrant," *O Oinountios* (July, 1927), 19–20.
² For a convenient summary of the disastrous Greek campaign in Asia Minor see A. A. Pallis, *Greece's Anatolia Venture and After* (London, 1937); Edward S. Forster, *A Short History of Modern Greece* (London, 1946), pp. 141–147.
³ A little insight into the problems of the returned immigrant was obtained from the files of the American Consulate in Athens. See letters of Wilbur J. Carr to Will L. Lowrie, Mar. 9, June 12, Aug. 2, 11, 1922.
⁴ Data issued by Greek Embassy in Washington.
⁵ Typical of the scattered articles giving some recognition to the returned immigrant was one by K. Tsaprali, "The Arcadian Immigrant and His

NOTES

Works" ("O Arkas Metanastis Kai To Ergon Tou"), *Arcadian Diary 1937* (Tripolis, 1937), pp. 85–86. Files of *Malebos* for 1922–1925 and *O Oinountios* for 1927–1928 were consulted in the Library of the Greek Parliament. Most of the critical comments about returned immigrants were obtained from native Greeks who often volunteered their observations.

[6] To the best of my knowledge C. M. Woodhouse, in his *Apple of Discord* (London, 1948), p. 106, is the only non-Greek to note the epithet "Brooklidhes" which the natives pinned on the returned Greek-American. For an account in Greek, see *Panarcadiake*, Aug. 1, 1954.

[7] A brief description of a returned Greek-American appeared in Kostas Paroritis, "E Orge Tou Amerikanou" ("The Wrath of the American") in F. Skokou, *National Diary, 1913* (*Ethnikon Emerologion, 1913*) (Athens, 1913), pp. 236–237. See also *Malebos*, V (July, 1925), 416.

[8] *Tenth Anniversary Edition of the National Herald* (*Dekaetris Ethnikou Kyrikos*), XI (Apr., 1925), 64–65; Charles E. Lloyd, "Modern Greece," *Cosmopolitan*, XXII (Apr., 1897), 587–598; *The Ahepa Magazine*, X (July–Aug., 1936), 10.

[9] *Malebos*, III (July, 1923), 123.

[10] Much of the spirit regarding the dependence of villagers on Greek-Americans to take their daughters, or those of their close relatives, in marriage, is revealed in a little sketch, "The Americans" ("E Amerikanoi"), *Malebos*, III (Apr., 1923), 83.

CHAPTER FOUR

ECONOMIC FORTUNES AND MISFORTUNES

[1] *California*, Jan. 31, 1920. For a brief account of the small market Greece furnished for agricultural equipment, see *Trade Information Bulletin*, no. 488, U.S. Department of Commerce (Washington, 1927), p. 9. For an account of the opportunities for automotive repairs in Greece, see *Trade Information Bulletin*, no. 482, U.S. Department of Commerce, pp. 26–27. In 1927 there were an estimated 7,000 cars in use in the Athens-Piraeus district.

[2] *Annual Report of the Commissioner General of Immigration, 1926* (Washington, 1926), pp. 204–205.

[3] *Commercial and Financial Chronicle*, CXIV (Apr. 15, 1922), 1590. See also the mimeographed "Statement by the Greek Delegate at the Twenty-fifth Meeting, Friday, June 13, 1952, before Provisional Inter-Governmental Committee for the Movement of Migrants from Europe," p. 2.

[4] *Commercial and Financial Chronicle*, CXIV (Apr. 15, 1922), 1590. See also New York *Times*, Apr. 5, 12, 14, 21, 1922; *Atlantis*, Apr. 22, 26–28, 1922. For a fuller account see *Trade Information Bulletin*, no. 68, U.S. Department of Commerce (Washington, 1922).

[5] *Commercial and Financial Chronicle*, CXIV (May 13, 1922), 2070.

[6] Wilbur J. Carr to Will L. Lowrie, Correspondence, American Consulate General, Athens, Greece, Part III, 1922. See also *Commercial and Financial Chronicle*, CXV (Dec. 30, 1922), 2849–2850.

[7] M. S. Eulambio, *The National Bank of Greece, a History of the Financial and Economic Evolution of Greece* (Athens, 1924), pp. 152–153; *Trade Information Bulletin*, no. 506, U.S. Department of Commerce (Washington, 1927), p. 17.

[8] *Commercial and Financial Chronicle*, CXVI (Apr. 7, 1923), 1477.

NOTES

⁹ *Ibid.*, CXXII (Jan. 9, 30, 1926), 131, 520–521; New York *Times*, Jan. 25, 1926; *Nea Apo Tin Hellada (News from Greece)*, Bank of Athens, Bulletin no. 1, Feb., 1926, p. 11. The "Public Debt in Greece," including summaries of the loans, is found in *Trade Information Bulletin*, no. 321, U.S. Department of Commerce (Washington, 1925).

¹⁰ John Metaxas, *Tessara Hronia Diakibernesseos (Four Years of Government)* (Athens, 1940), I, 72–73.

¹¹ "Remittances of Greek Immigrants," *Monthly Record of Immigration*, International Labor Office, no. 50 (Nov., 1926), 462.

¹² "Report by MSA Field Representative John Asher in Greece on 'The 120 Workers on the Island of Karpathos,'" dated Sept. 24, 1952. A list of the names of ninety-two workers and a brief statement of their economic status accompany this typed report.

¹³ Eliot G. Mears, *Greece Today* (Stanford, 1929), p. 175.

¹⁴ New York *Times*, Nov. 13, 1953; *Analysis of the Social Security System*, Part 2, 83d Cong., 1st sess. (Washington, 1953), pp. 81–91.

¹⁵ Milwaukee *Journal*, July 11, 1954.

¹⁶ *Ibid.*

¹⁷ "Report by MSA Field Representative John Asher in Greece...." dated Sept. 24, 1952.

CHAPTER SIX

THE REPATRIATED AND THEIR CRITICS

¹ *O Xeniteumenos*, Jan. 17, 1935.

² Dionysius Sakellari, *Triumphant Altars and Distressed Souls (Vome Thriamvon Kai Thlimennes Psyches)* (Athens, 1930), pp. 207–218; *American Legion, Department of Greece*, Bulletin no. 5 (*Amerikaniki Legioni, Tmemata Hellados*, Deltion arithmos 5), Athens, Apr. 1, 1953; Willie S. Ethridge, *It's Greek To Me* (New York, 1948), p. 23.

³ For noncritical material on the AHEPA in Greece, see Sakellari, *op. cit.*, pp. 221–226; *The Ahepa Magazine* (July–Aug., 1947), 47–48. Among the pictures of Greek-Americans in Greece was one of Samuel Insull, American utilities magnate who visited the Ahepans on the *Byron*. See *Menaeos Eikonographimenos Ethnikos Kyrix*, XIX (Mar., 1933), 34.

CHAPTER SEVEN

SOME GREEK-AMERICAN INFLUENCES

¹ *Atlantis*, Feb. 14, 1907; Jan. 13, Dec. 24, 1908; July 6, 1912; *To Kratos*, Aug. 26, 1907; *Greek Star*, July 31, 1908; *California*, Mar. 27, 1920; *Malebos*, III (Apr., 1922), 90; *Monthly Illustrated Atlantis (Menea Eikonographimeni Atlantis)*, I (June, 1910), 31; *Report of the Treasurer to the Officers, Directors and Members of the Greek War Relief Association, Inc.*, Nov. 2, 1950, especially pp. 6–21 inclusive.

² Eliot G. Mears, "The Unique Position in Greek Trade of Emigrant Remittances," *Quarterly Journal of Economics*, XXXVII (May, 1923), 539; "Report by MSA Field Representative John Asher in Greece on 'The 120 Workers on the Island of Karpathos,'" dated Sept. 24, 1952; *Reports of the Immigration Commission*, Vol. IV: *Emigration Conditions in Europe*,

NOTES

U.S. 61st Cong., 3d sess., S. Doc. 748 (Washington, 1911), pp. 397, 412–414 (hereafter cited as *Emigration Conditions in Europe*).

³ *Emigration Conditions in Europe*, pp. 397–398. See also C. F. Speare, "What America Pays Europe for Immigrant Labor," *North American Review*, vol. 187 (Jan., 1908), 106–116; J. W. Gregory, *Human Migration and the Future* (Philadelphia, 1927), pp. 30–32.

⁴ *Emigration Conditions in Europe*, p. 398.

⁵ *Ibid.*, p. 413.

⁶ Although most remittances received in Greece came from the United States, there were smaller ones from Australia, South America, and various points on the European continent.

A comparison of several sources on remittances shows some discrepancies, which the reader should keep in mind. The figures for 1910 to 1936 inclusive were obtained from the National Bank of Greece, *Economic Yearbook of Greece, 1938 (Ekonomike Epeteris Tis Hellados, Etos Dekaton, 1938)*, Part II (Athens, 1939), p. 174. Figures for 1937 to 1939 inclusive were obtained from a pamphlet published by the Greek office of Information, *Greece, Basic Statistics* (London, 1949), p. 20. Figures from 1945 to 1950 were obtained from a leaflet put out by the Monthly Statement Bank of Athens, *Greece To-Day*, p. 4. Compare the above figures with those cited by Eliot G. Mears, *Greece Today* (Stanford, 1929), pp. 195–196. See also *Report to the Council on Greece*, League of Nations, Financial Committee (Geneva, 1933), p. 18 and the explanations offered for the fluctuations in remittances. See also *Report on the Industrial and Economic Situation in Greece*, Department of Overseas Trade (London, 1927), p. 42.

⁷ "Remittances of Greek Immigrants," *Monthly Record of Immigration*, International Labor Office, no. 50 (Nov., 1926), 426; *Trade Information Bulletin*, U.S. Department of Commerce, no. 506 (Washington, 1927), p. 17.

⁸ *Report of the Treasurer to the Officers, Directors and Members of the Greek War Relief Association, Inc.*, Nov. 2, 1950. Mimeograph material in files of Greek War Relief Ass'n, Athens, Greece. See also *Atlantis*, June 29, 1952.

⁹ U.S. *Consular Reports, 1900*, pp. 388–389; *1907*, p. 403; *1908*, pp. 13, 233; *1909*, p. 180. See *E Kathemerini*, Mar. 6, 9, 1924, for Greek advertisements of American automobiles and automotive products. See also *Nea Ephemeris*, Mar. 11, 1912. A Greek-American who had just returned from the United States, where he had worked in several large shoe factories, was advertising his readiness to accept orders to make shoes based on his American experiences.

¹⁰ *Panhellenios Kratos*, Oct. 23, 1908; Stathis Speliotopoulos, *History of the National Bank (Historia Tis Ethnikis Trapezis)* (Athens, 1949), pp. 102, 132–133.

¹¹ The first issue of *News from Greece (Nea Apo Tin Hellada)* appeared in Feb., 1926.

¹² M. S. Eulambio, *The National Bank of Greece* (Athens, 1924), pp. 152–153, on the distrust created by the forced government loans among Greeks in the United States. *Ethnikos Kyrix*, Nov. 26, 1922, reported that the Bank of Athens was the first Greek bank to have a branch in the United States, and the only one at that time.

¹³ Highly illustrative of this effort was a brochure issued by the National Bank of Greece to advertise its many features serving Greek nationals who lived abroad. See *1951 The Year for Greeks Living Abroad* (*1951 Etos*

NOTES

Apodemou Hellenismou), especially pp. 1–6. This year was advertised as "Home-coming Year" for all Greeks residing in other countries. See also *The Ahepa Magazine*, X (July–Aug., 1936), 8–9; *O Xeniteumenos*, Jan. 17, 1935.

[14] *To Kratos*, Aug. 26, 1907; *Menea Eikonographimeni Atlantis*, I (June, 1910), 310. The Federation of Greek-American Associations was formed on May 10, 1936, "to render service to Greek-Americans and act as the connecting link of the Greek and American people" (*The Ahepa Magazine*, X [July–Aug., 1936], 10).

[15] Popular cafes operated by Greek-Americans in Athens were Zonars, the Piccadilly, and the Astoria.

[16] Antonios Saousopoulos, "The Influence of Laborers Returning from the United States on Greek Syndicalism" ("E Epidrasis Ergaton Epanelthonton ex Amerikis is Ton Hellinikon Syndicalismon"), three-page typescript dated Athens, Greece, Mar. 18, 1953.

[17] *Atlantis*, Nov. 7, 1908; Mar. 20, 1909.

[18] W. Byford-Jones, *The Greek Trilogy* (London, 1945), pp. 93–95.

[19] *The Financial World* (London), Mar. 23, 1931.

[20] The vote tabulations do not clarify the situation as much as might be expected. The elections of November 16, 1952, indicated that Nicholas Plastiras, head of the left-of-center party, EPEK, scored a heavy vote in the Salonika area. He ran second to Alex. Papagos, head of the rightist ticket, but the EDA party, even farther left than Plastiras, made an impressive showing. See *E Kathemerini*, Nov. 17, 18, 1952; *Athens News*, Nov. 18, 1952.

[21] Regarding the Greeks of Egypt, see Athanase G. Politis, *L'hellenisme et l'Egypte moderne*, Tome 1–2 (Paris, 1929–1930). Volume 2 stresses the role played by the Greeks in developing modern Egypt.

[22] *To Kratos*, Mar. 23, 1914.

[23] See Toynbee quotation in N. Forbes, A. J. Toynbee, D. Mitrany, and D. G. Hogarth, *The Balkans, a History of Bulgaria, Serbia, Greece, Rumania, Turkey* (Oxford University Press, 1915), p. 249, quoted by E. G. Mears in *Greece Today*, p. vii. See also Demetrios N. Koufos, "The Return of the One Living Abroad" ("O Yerismos Tou Xeniteumenou"), *Malebos*, III (July, 1923), 123; *O Oinountios*, July, 1927, p. 80; Gregory, *op. cit.*, pp. 30–32; *Emigration Conditions in Europe*, pp. 414–415. See also *The Ahepa Magazine*, X (July–Aug., 1936), 10, on the encouragement given to community cleanliness and beautification by Greek-Americans.

SOURCES AND BIBLIOGRAPHY

As suggested in the Preface, the findings presented in this study are a composite result of research in the field and in various libraries in both Greece and the United States. The author questioned at length approximately 70 repatriates in Greece and talked to about 120 other persons, including former immigrants, Americans stationed in Greece, and Greeks who never emigrated to the United States. The Appendix to this book contains a sample copy of the questionnaire employed in interviewing repatriates. The answers to the questionnaires and the records of the more numerous interviews are in the author's personal files.

Efforts to locate manuscript materials dealing with repatriates met with little success. Apparently neither diaries nor letters, nor indeed any written materials that might be of use to future historians, were preserved. There is also a dearth of articles about repatriates in periodicals. As a rule, Greek-Americans led a humdrum existence, day in, day out, in the United States. They had little appreciation for anything except material values, and artistic, creative, literary, or intellectual aspirations were beyond the range of their interests.

Unfortunately, the partisan and highly individualized Greek press also failed to give the repatriates serious attention. When they began to come back from America in substantial numbers during 1907–1908, the press was chiefly concerned with publicizing the unfavorable aspects of emigration. During 1912–1913, the years of the Balkan Wars, Greek military victories and aspirations overshadowed everything else in importance. Pretty much the same appears to have been true after the First World War, when rampant Panhellenism reached its peak, and the Greek debacle of 1922 in Asia Minor threw the nation into mourning. The preponderance of crucial domestic and foreign problems facing the small country of Greece reduced the repatriate to the status of a truly "forgotten man."

BIBLIOGRAPHY

There were few Greek government reports bearing on immigration. Of the two consulted, the more valuable is *A Study on Immigration with Suggested Legislation (Meleti Meta Schediou Nomou Peri Metanasteuseos)* by Emmanuel Repouli, published in Athens in 1912. Repouli at the time was minister of the interior. Less important is *Emigration from Greece, a Report of the Committee of Parliament (E Ex Hellados Metanasteusis, E Ekthesis Tis Epitropis Tis Voulis)*, published in Athens in 1906. Both are available in the Library of the Greek Parliament in Athens, which is well stocked with materials on contemporary Greek affairs.

Greek statistical data leave much to be desired. In 1929 E. G. Mears wrote, "The statistics used should more properly be called figures, because of the much marked tendency of Greeks, in both official and private life, to regard statistics merely as tools to prove certain contentions or otherwise influence particular situations. Accuracy of figures and accuracy of statement do not appear to the typical Greek as matters of particular merit or concern...." Major exceptions to this were the monthly and annual reports of several of the Greek banks, especially the National Bank of Greece, the Bank of Greece, the Bank of Athens, and the Agricultural Bank of Greece. The student with a command of modern Greek will find *Economic Yearbook of Greece, Tenth Year, 1938 (Ekonomike Epeteris Tis Hellados, Etos Dekaton, 1938)* (Athens, 1939) very helpful. Issued by the National Bank of Greece, it contains a great deal of invaluable general information and many statistical data that go back to the early 1920's and even to the late nineteenth century.

Most helpful among United States government documents were the *Consular Reports* from 1900 to 1910; *Reports of the Immigration Commission*, Vol. IV: *Emigration Conditions in Europe*, U.S. 61st Cong., 3d sess., S. Doc. 748 (Washington, 1911); and *Statistical Review of Immigration, 1820–1910*, S. Doc. 756 (Washington, 1911). For statistical data, see the *Annual Reports of the Commissioner General of Immigration* from 1908 to 1932 and the *Statistical Abstract of the United States* from 1932 to 1952. Of some value is the *Report of the*

BIBLIOGRAPHY

Commission on the Problem of Immigration in Massachusetts (Boston, 1914). The U.S. Department of Commerce has issued several bulletins that were useful. One by P. L. Edwards, "Operation and Consequences of the Greek Forced Loan Law," *Trade Information Bulletin*, no. 68 (Washington, 1922) is the best treatment of the subject in the English language. Accounts of the law appear in the *Commercial and Financial Chronicle* and the *London Economist* for 1922. The indexes of both the *London Economist* and the New York *Times* yielded additional details. *Trade Information Bulletins*, nos. 321, 472, and 506, contain materials on the Greek public debt, business practices, and methods of trade finance and exchange.

Among newspapers published in Greece which proved helpful were *E Sphaira* (Piraeus), 1907–1908; *To Kratos* (Athens), 1907–1915; *E Kathemerini* (Athens), 1922, 1924; *Nea Ephemeris* (Irakleion, Crete), Apr. 8, 1911–Dec. 29, 1912; and *O Xeniteumenos* (Athens), Jan. 17, 31, 1935. The first three are available in the Library of the Greek Parliament, *Nea Ephemeris* is in the Public Library of Irakleion, and the two issues of *O Xeniteumenos* are the personal property of Mr. Stavros Skopeteas, an assistant librarian in the Library of the Greek Parliament. Skopeteas, the son of a repatriated immigrant, was trained as a lawyer.

There were several Greek periodicals other than newspapers that were helpful. A new bimonthly publication, *Panarkadiake* (Tripolis, Greece), has been circulating among Arcadians in the United States since 1953. It currently serves as an adopted spokesman for the Pan-Arcadian Federation. Greek publications throwing light on the ties between the provinces and Greeks in the United States are *O Oinountios* (Piraeus), 1927–1928, and *Malebos* (Athens), 1922–1925. Both made frequent reference to repatriated Greek-Americans and are available in the Library of the Greek Parliament.

Indispensable to any student of the Greek immigrant are the files of the Greek language press in the United States. Most valuable are *Atlantis* (New York), 1895 to the present; *National Herald* (New York), 1915 to the present; *Greek Star* (Chicago),

BIBLIOGRAPHY

1904 to the present; and *California* (San Francisco), 1907 to the present. The first two are daily and Sunday publications; the last two are weeklies. *Atlantis,* the royalist mouthpiece, was consulted for the periods 1895-1897 and 1907-1914; the *National Herald,* the Venezelist organ, for 1922; the *Greek Star* for the two years 1907-1908; and *California* for the years 1907-1910 and 1917-1920. *Atlantis* and the *National Herald* were also issued monthly as the *Illustrated Monthly Atlantis* (*Menea Eikonographimeni Atlantis*), 1910-1916 and 1919-1921, and the *Illustrated Monthly National Herald* (*Menaeos Eikonographimenos Ethnikos Kyrix*), Jan.-June, 1916, 1921, 1923, 1924, 1927, 1930-1935. The tenth anniversary edition of the latter, published in 1925, has much pertinent material on Greeks in the United States. A partial file of *Panhellenios,* from Apr. 7 to Dec. 31, 1908, is preserved in the Benaki Library, Athens, a valuable depository for materials on Greece. *Panhellenios* was published in New York City but is not available in the United States.

As general sources on immigration in the English language, three books of varying quality are available: Henry Pratt Fairchild, *Greek Immigration to the United States* (New Haven, 1911); J. P. Xenides, *The Greeks in America* (New York, 1922); and Thomas Burgess, *Greeks in America* (Boston, 1913). The most valuable part of Fairchild's book deals with the economic causes of immigration. Many portions of the work, however, are impressionistic or hostile, and contain reactions characteristic of Americans when first exposed to a different culture. The Xenides book, though marred by superficiality and oversympathy for the immigrants, discusses in abbreviated form topics avoided by Fairchild. Xenides was born of Greek parents in Asia Minor and came into close contact with Greek immigrants in the United States; he is understanding, charitable, and even apologetic. Almost eulogistic in tone is the book written by Burgess, a Protestant clergyman whose sympathies are undeniably with the immigrant. Ephemeral and less valuable because of its exaggerated Greek patriotism is *Hellenism in America,* by S. G. Canoutas, published in New York in 1918. One of the few

BIBLIOGRAPHY

books written in English but published in Athens (in 1899) is *America and Greece,* by Konstantinos D. Maniakes.

For general information on Greece, Vol. XIV of the *Great Hellenic Encyclopaedia (Megale Helleniki Enkeklopaedia)* (Athens, 1930) is very useful. For specific information on Greek-Americans, the most exhaustive general account written in Greek (despite its English title) is Baumbi Malafouris, *Greeks in America, 1528-1948* (New York, 1948). It has a good bibliography, but suffers because of its uncritical writing and because its publication depended on subscriptions from various Greek-Americans. An invaluable volume, *Greek Immigration, with an Introduction by Andreas M. Andreadou (Helleniki Metanasteusis, Meta Prologou Andreas M. Andreadou)* (Athens, 1917), was prepared by the students of Andreas Mich. Andreadou, perhaps the foremost Greek economist of his day. Containing essays on emigration from all parts of Greece, it is indispensable for a study of the local conditions that aggravated the exodus to the United States. More popular in approach is the work of Michael A. Dendia, *Greek Colonies around the World (Hellenikai Parikiai Ana Ton Kosmon)* (Athens, 1919), which treats of emigration to Russia, Rumania, Egypt, the United States, and other parts of the world.

Other helpful secondary sources in Greek were the following: N. Gkortzi, *America and the Americans (Ameriki Kai Amerikani)* (Athens, 1907?), presents a brief account of the United States and its people for the general Greek reader; Elias I. Janetis, *His Eminence, the Immigrant (E Autou Megaliotis, O Metanastis)* (New York, 1946), contains a series of short humorous narratives based on actual experience; Alexis Krikou, *The Status of Hellenism in America (E Theshis Tou Hellenismou En Ameriki)* (Athens, 1915), describes the conditions confronting immigrants to the United States; E. S. Lekoude, *The Immigrants (E Metanastai)* (Athens, 1903), is one of the first general accounts to appear in Greece; G. M. Marinou, *The Nation of Wealth (To Kratos Tou Ploutou)* (Athens, 1904), supplements Lekoude; Man. A. Triantafillidi, *Greeks of America (Hellenes*

BIBLIOGRAPHY

Tis Amerikes) is a popular and sympathetic, though sketchy, treatment by a Greek philologist and educator who traveled in the United States in 1940, just before the Second World War. Gkortzi, Lekoude, and Marinou were all published in Athens by the Society for the Publication of Beneficial Books.

Studies on various phases of immigration, but emphasizing Greek economic life, are: Demetriou N. Mihalopoulou, *The Politics of Living Abroad (E Politiki Tis Apodemias)* (Athens, 1938); Stathis Speliotopoulos, *History of the National Bank (Historia Tis Ethnikis Trapezis)* (Athens, 1949); Xenophon Zolota, *Currency and Exchange Phenomena in Greece, 1910–1927 (Nomismetika Kai Synallagmatika Phenomena En Helladi, 1910–1927)* (Athens, 1928). The last volume was written by a prominent young Greek economist.

Secondary works in the English language covering various aspects of Greek life are numerous; there are more books of this kind for Greece than for most of the Balkan countries. For the general student Eliot G. Mears, *Greece Today* (Stanford, 1929), is indispensable. Percy F. Martin, *Greece of the Twentieth Century* (London, 1913) appeared when the emigration movement to the United States was at its peak, and contains a very helpful picture of social, political, and economic conditions during this crucial period in the nation's history. A. A. Pallis, *Greece's Anatolia Venture and After* (London, 1937), is helpful for an understanding of events that influenced domestic and foreign policy after the humiliating Greek defeat of 1922 in Asia Minor.

Information about Greeks in the United States is also found in F. J. Brown and J. S. Roucek, *Our Racial and National Minorities* (New York, 1937), and in Theodore Saloutos, "The Greeks in the United States," *South Atlantic Quarterly*, XLIV (Jan., 1945), 69–81. The latter was reprinted in William Hamilton, ed., *Fifty Years of the* South Atlantic Quarterly (Durham, 1952), pp. 306–318.

The subject of remittances is dealt with in the International Labor Office's *Monthly Record of Immigration*, no. 50 (Nov., 1926), 426; in E. G. Mears, "Unique Position in Greek Trade of Emigrant Remittances," *Quarterly Journal of Economics*,

XXXVII (May, 1923), 535-540; and in C. F. Speare, "What America Pays Europe for Immigrant Labor," *North American Review*, CLXXXVII (Jan., 1908), 106-116.

An essay by Theodore Saloutos, "Greece and Recovery," *Yale Review*, XLIII (June, 1954), 535-547, portrays general conditions in Greece after the Second World War.

INDEX

Agriculture: in Greece, 3; shunned by immigrants in United States, 12
American Hellenic Educational Progressive Association (AHEPA): in United States, 26; in Greece, 113–114
American influences: abroad, vii; in Greece, 117–131
American Legion: officer of, on repatriation, 49; in Greece, 113
Assimilation, dangers of, to Greece, 31–32
Athens, repatriates in, 38, 48, 60–61, 88–90, 91, 131
Atlantis: as royalist daily, 27; on Lambros Coromilas, 34; on Greco-Turkish War, 1897, 35; on Balkan Wars, 38; conducts ideological campaign, 126–127

Balkan Wars: returned immigrants on, xii, 37–40; Greek-Americans poorly prepared for, 39; Greater Greece and, 59
Bank failures, repatriates and, 104
Benefactors: of Greece, 26; repatriate role as, 68–69
Business: complaints regarding ethics of, 71–72; adjustments in Greece, 80–81; contrast in methods of, 104–105

Capital tax, 76–77
Cities, repatriates in Greek, 61
Coffeehouses, 23–25
Constantine, King: *Atlantis,* mouthpiece of, in United States, 27; and Greater Greece, 40
Crete, repatriates in, 49, 60, 65
Critics: repatriates as, 104–106; repatriates as targets of, 106–108; evaluation of, 108
Customs office in Greece, 58–59

Destination: of immigrants, 11; of repatriates, 60–61

Discrimination: experienced by immigrants, 19; references to, by repatriates, 111
Distinctions: social, in Greece, 102; repatriate observations on, 103
Dowry: immigration and, 7; repatriate on, 72–73

Eccentricities of repatriates, 64, 69
Enemy agents, Greek, in United States, 27
Exploitation: labor agents and, 15–16; *padrone* system and, 16–17; ticket agents and, 16–17

Family expectations, repatriates and, 66–70
Farming, avoided by Greeks in United States, 12
Field work: in United States, viii; in Greece, xi–xiii
Food: immigrant cuisine, 18; American products in Greece, 121; influence of, on Greek habits, 125
Forced loan: in Greece, 1922, 75; reaction of Greek-Americans, 76–78; in Greece, 1926, 77; remittances and, 119
Frustrations of repatriates, 91–92, 94, 99–100, 115–116

Greece, Greater: repatriates and Balkan Wars, 59; hopes for, frustrated, 74–75
Greek-American Progressive Association (GAPA): in the United States, 26; in Greece, 113–114
Greek Orthodox Church: importance of, to immigrant, 21–23; politics and, 22–23
Greeks: in United States before 1900, 1–2; origin of immigrants, 2; attraction of, to United States, 3–5; youth, 6; in Ottoman Empire, 8–9; in United States about 1900, 11
Greek societies, 25, 35
Greek War Relief, 117

INDEX

Housekeeping, immigrants and cooperative, 19

Image of United States: by Greeks, 3, 28, 69, 94; by repatriates after 1940, 109–111
Immigration: reasons for, 2–9; relative freedom of, 1897–1912, 35; United States policy criticized, 111–112; during World War II and aftermath, 130–131
Impressions: early, of United States, 14; repatriate, of United States, 64–66, 93–95
Influences: American abroad, vii; repatriates and, 89–91, 98; of American Legion, 117–121; of Greek-American commercial relations, 117–121; of good times in United States and Greece, 118; of Greek banking in United States, 121–122; psychological, 123; on public improvements, 123–124; on spirit of progress, 123–124; of tourist agencies, 123–124; on practical outlook, 124; on eating habits, 125; on education of young, 125–126; ideological, 126–127; of Greek-Americans on resistance movement, 127–128; general observations on, 130–131
Insecurity: and crossing Atlantic, 10–11; discrimination and, 19; rationalization caused by, 19–20; strange surroundings and, 20; company of compatriots and, 20–21
Intellectuals: among immigrants, 13–14; among repatriates, 53
Interviews: strength and weaknesses of method of, xiv–xv; number of, 143
Investments, repatriates and, 78–79, 88–91, 93–97, 100, 101

Karagiozis in United States, 25, 95–96
Karpathos, repatriates on island of, 60, 79, 86

Labor agent, immigrant and, 4
Language difficulties, 14–15, 19
Library resources, Greek, vii, 143

Marriage: opportunity for, and immigration, 7; preference for own nationality in, 40–41, 90, 98; eligibility of repatriate for, 72–73
Mears, Eliot G., on Greek business methods, 80
Metaxas, John: debt- and interest-scaling decrees of, 77; and "golden age" of Greece, 89
Military service: immigration imperils national defense, 5; immigrants desire to escape from, 5–6, 92; Greek response to, 6–7; repatriates and, 59–60
Mutual Security Administration, 121
Mytilene, repatriates in, xiii, 39, 101

National Herald (liberal Republican daily), 27
Nationalism, Greek: revival of, 7–8; evidences of abroad, 26; and Spyros Matsoukas, 36–37; and "Greater Greece," 40, 74–75; weakening of, 54–55; repatriates and, 98–99
Nationality, Greek conception of, 9
Navpaktos, repatriates in, 78, 97–98
Nea Hellas, returning immigrants aboard the, ix–xi
New immigration, national and geographic origins of, 1

Occupations, immigrant: in United States, 13, 17; bootblacks, 16; hairdressers, 88–89
Organizations, Greek-American, 113–114

Padrone system, Greek version of, 16–17
Panhellenic Union: origins of, 35–36; and Balkan Wars, 40
Panhellenios, rival of *Atlantis*, 27
Patras, repatriates in, xii, 60–61
Peloponnesus, repatriates in, 41–42, 60, 65, 79, 91–92
Press, Greek-American, 27

Reactions toward repatriates, xiv, 62–64
Reformist influences: repatriates and, 109; spirit of progress and, 123–124

INDEX

Religion, Greek Orthodox, 21–23
Remittances: Greek-Americans and, 117–121; reasons for decline of, 119–120; statistical table of, 120
Repatriates: economic status of, 53–54; apprehensions of, 54–55; weakening of national spirit and, 55; anticipations of, 55–56, 62–63; emotional state of, 57–58; from other countries than United States, 61–62; reactions in Greece toward, 62–63; contented, 83–84; aged, 114–115; children of, 115; contrasted and compared, 129–130; as "forgotten men," 143
Repatriation: means of encouraging, 29–32; statistics on, 30, 49–52; Panic of 1907 and, 32–34; Balkan Wars and, 37–40; family ties and, 41–44; and preservation of customs and traditions, 45; climate as a factor in, 46; health and, 46; Great Depression and, 47–48; preference for simpler life shown by, 47, 101–102; cheaper living costs and, 48; naturalized citizens and, 51; sex and, 51; patriotism a factor in, 99; generalizations on wisdom of, 115
Reverses, repatriate: financial losses caused by, 93, 97, 100, 101, 103; family involvements and, 95; force reappraisal of United States, 109–111
Rhodes, repatriates on island of, 60, 67, 79

Salonika, repatriates in, 79, 92–93
Shopkeepers, immigrant, and long hours, 17–18

Social activities, immigrants and, 21–26
Social Science Research Council, viii
Social Security: repatriates under, 84–86; repatriates on island of Karpathos seek, 86
Statistics: on Greeks in United States, 9–10; quality of, in Greece, 144
Steamship companies: between United States and Greece, 10; promote Greek patriotism, 123

Thessaly, repatriates in, ix–x, xii–xiii
Tripolis, repatriates in, 39, 47, 60–61, 65

United States: and aid to Greece, 99, 117; criticisms of, 111

Venizelos, Eleutherios: *National Herald*, mouthpiece of, in United States, 27; Lambros Coromilas in cabinet of, 37
Villages: repatriates in, 61; readjustment problems in, 70–72

Women: and immigration, 7; immigrants seek mates of own nationality, 40–41
World War I: repatriation after, 42, 50–51, 59, 74; veterans of, in Greece, 85–86; American Legion in Greece, 114
World War II: effects of, on repatriates, 81–82; status of repatriates prior to, 83; immigration from Greece after, 130

www.ingramcontent.com/pod-product-compliance
Lightning Source LLC
Chambersburg PA
CBHW021710230426
43668CB00008B/791